The Unchanging Christ

The Unchanging Christ

Twelve Sermons
from a Master Preacher

H. A. Ironside

LOIZEAUX
Neptune, New Jersey

THE UNCHANGING CHRIST
by H. A. Ironside

First Edition, 1934
Revised Edition, 1942

A Publication of Loizeaux Brothers, Inc.,
A Nonprofit Organization Devoted to the Lord's Work
and to the Spread of His Truth

All rights reserved.
No part of this book may be reproduced or transmitted
in any form or by any means, electronic or mechanical,
including photocopying and recording,
or by any information storage and retrieval system,
without the prior written permission of the publisher,
except in the case of brief quotations embodied
in critical articles or reviews.

Unless otherwise indicated, Scripture quotations are taken from
the King James version of the Bible.

Library of Congress Cataloging-in-Publication Data

ISBN: 0-87213-443-1

Printed in the United States of America
10 9 8 7 6 5 4 3 2 1

Contents

1. The Unchanging Christ 7
   Acts 1:9-11
2. Ungodly Sinners Justified 15
   Romans 4:4-5
3. Saved by His Life 27
   Romans 5:10
4. The Sacrifice Bound to the Altar 35
   Psalm 118:27
5. The Message of Pentecost 41
   Acts 2:22-36
6. Consistent Christian Behavior 51
   Deuteronomy 22:8-12
7. The Priesthood of All Believers 61
   Hebrews 13:15-16
8. The Presentation of First Fruits 71
   Deuteronomy 26; Hebrews 13:15-16
9. How Pontius Pilate Lost His Soul 79
   John 19:10-16
10. The Folly of Procrastination 91
    Acts 24:25
11. Prophecy, An Outstanding Proof of the Inspiration of the Bible 101
    2 Peter 1:21
12. "Where Is the Promise of His Coming?" 111
    2 Peter 3:1-9

CHAPTER ONE

The Unchanging Christ

And when he had spoken these things, while they beheld, he was taken up; and a cloud received him out of their sight. And while they looked stedfastly toward heaven as he went up, behold, two men stood by them in white apparel; Which also said, Ye men of Galilee, why stand ye gazing up into heaven? this same Jesus, which is taken up from you into heaven, shall so come in like manner as ye have seen him go into heaven.

(ACTS 1:9-11)

I want you to notice especially those precious words, "This same Jesus." Men often talk of needing a new Christ for a new age. In a recent book, which has been widely read, the writer states that a changing order demands a fresh revelation of God, that we cannot think of any past revelation as "the faith once for all delivered to the saints." He declares that inasmuch as times change, people change, and our viewpoints change, it is not to be supposed that the Christ of nineteen hundred years ago will meet the needs of men today. God reveals Himself in different ways and He may have another revelation of Himself which will soon break upon us making all previous ones obsolete!

It is very common to hear people using that kind of language today but when we turn to the blessed Book of God, we find that our Lord Jesus Christ is God's last word to men. In Hebrews 1:1-2 we read, "God, who at sundry times and in divers manners [in many ways] spake in time past unto the fathers by the prophets, Hath in these last days spoken unto us by his Son, whom he hath appointed heir of all things, by whom also he made the worlds." The word translated, "worlds" there is the customary word for "ages," and that verse may be translated, "By whom also he fitted the ages together." Christ is the beginning, Christ is the end, and Christ is the center of all the ages. "Who being the brightness of his glory, and the express image of his person, and upholding all things by the word of his power, when he had by himself purged our sins, sat down on the right hand of the Majesty on high" (Hebrews 1:3). And there He sits today, the same blessed Savior that He was when here on earth.

In the last chapter of this Epistle we have those wonderful words, "Jesus Christ the same yesterday and today, and for ever" (Hebrews 13:8). "Jesus Christ the same *yesterday*"—that carries us back to the long ages before He became incarnate. You and I began to be when we were born into this world. It was otherwise with our Lord Jesus Christ. He did not begin to live when He was born of the blessed virgin Mary, He simply changed His clothing as it were. He who had been in the form of God, who thought it not robbery to be equal with God, divested Himself of the garments of glory that had been His from all eternity, clothed Himself in a body of flesh and blood, stooped in grace to become a servant, as servant became not an angel but a man, and as man humbled Himself and became obedient unto death. And such a death, that of the cross! He was the same in the past eternity. In John 16:28 we hear Him say, "I came forth from the Father and am come into the world: again, I leave the world, and go to the Father." There you have Him in the past. He came forth from the Father; He dwelt in the Father's bosom throughout the interminable ages of the past.

"In the beginning was the Word." That is, when everything that ever had beginning began, "the Word *was*." Not, "the Word began." This was an unbeginning beginning. "The Word was with God, and the Word was God. The same was in the beginning with God. All things were made by him; and without him was not anything made that was made. In him was life; and the life was the light of men." Notice the seven things that are predicated of Him in regard to the past, that "yesterday" of Hebrews 13. First, His eternal existence—"In the beginning was the Word." Second, His distinct personality—"The Word was *with* God." Third, His true and perfect Deity—"The Word *was* God." Fourth, the unchangeableness of His personal relationship to the Father—"The same was in the beginning with God." Fifth, His full creatorial glory—"All things were made by him; and without him was not anything made that was made." Sixth, all life had its source in Him—"In him was life." Seventh, all light comes from Him—"The life was the light of men." This is the One who came in grace into this world, assumed a servant's form, passed angels by, and became a man for our redemption.

Do we need a different Christ? Where will we find Him? God Himself has already come down to us and there is none higher than He to come.

> No angel could our place have taken,
> Highest of the high though he;
> The loved One, on the cross forsaken,
> Was one of the Godhead Three!

We look for no other Christ; there can be none other. God has been fully told out in Him. I believed that is involved in the expression: "In the beginning was the Word"—"The Logos." I wonder sometimes whether the Spirit of God did not intend this message given through John, to be the answer to the yearning cry of Plato and his followers throughout the Greek-speaking world. You remember that Plato, dazed, amazed, as he thought of the great mysteries of life, death and eternity, said on one occasion to that little group in Athens discussing these questions: "It may be that some day there will come forth from God a Word, a Logos, who will reveal all mysteries and make everything plain." And the Spirit of God, through the apostle John, said, "Yes, and He has come, the Logos was made flesh, became flesh, and dwelt among us, and we beheld His glory, the glory as of the only begotten of the Father, full of grace and truth."

Jesus Christ the same yesterday and Jesus Christ the same *today*; for having by Himself made purification for sins He has been raised from the dead by the glory of the Father. I wonder if you have ever noticed that the resurrection of our Lord Jesus Christ is attributed to every person of the Holy Trinity. We read in one instance that the Father raised Him from the dead; we read again that He was quickened by the Spirit; and then we hear Him saying, "Destroy this temple, and in three days I will raise it up." The Father raised Him from the dead, the Spirit raised Him from the dead, and the Son raised Himself from the dead. He said, "I have power to lay down my life and I have power to take it again." So intimate is the relationship subsisting between the three persons of the adorable Trinity that the one person does not act apart from the other. As Christ walked here on earth, the Father walked here also, and now that He has gone back to the Father He says, "I will send the Comforter;" but He also says, "If any man hear my voice, and open the door, I will come in to him, and will sup with him." By the reception of the Holy Spirit we now receive the Father and the Son. How wonderfully are we blessed! When our Savior comes again, God is coming to take control of things in this world and the Holy Spirit will be poured out upon all flesh. Father, Son and Holy Spirit in council in the past eternity; Father, Son, and Holy Spirit working out our salvation here on earth; Father, Son, and Holy Spirit bringing in the glory by and by when the long period of man's trial is over, when the kingdom is fully established, and the Lord Jesus Christ abides forevermore the One in whom the Father and Spirit as well as the Son are fully displayed, for He is the image of the invisible God.

In John 17 the Lord Jesus Christ was addressing the Father in His great high priestly prayer, and He said, "And now, O Father, glorify thou me with thine own self with the glory which I had with thee before the world was." He came from that glory into the degradation and humiliation of that which resulted in the cross, and now He has gone back to that glory but He remains a man in glory still. Does your soul get hold of that? Some Christians have lost the blessedness of it; they think Christ is no longer the man Christ Jesus that He was when here on earth, but Scripture says, There is "one mediator between God and men, the man Christ Jesus" (1 Timothy 2:5). And as the man in glory He is seated on the Father's throne, waiting until the day of His triumph when His enemies shall be made His footstool.

> When He comes, our glorious King,
> All His ransomed home to bring,
> Then anew this song we'll sing;
> 'Hallelujah! What a Saviour!'
> (Philip P. Bliss)

For the One who is coming back is Jesus Christ who is "the same yesterday and today and forever."

"This same Jesus which is taken up from you into heaven, shall so come in like manner as ye have seen him go into heaven." Away with the ridiculous errorists who tell us that Christ will never come back again as a man, that He only exists now as a part of the all-pervading spirit of the universe! He who walked on earth as the lowly man of Galilee, knelt in agony in Gethsemane's garden, cried in anguish from the cross, "My

God, my God, why hast thou forsaken me?" later surrendered His spirit in peace to the Father as He exclaimed, "It is finished"! He who was raised from the dead, walked for forty wonderful days among His disciples and then led them out one day to the Mount of Olives, as far as Bethany, was suddenly parted from them and ascended up and up until a cloud, the royal chariot of Heaven, came down and received Him out of their sight and wafted Him away to the Father's house from which He had come—this same Jesus will be unchanged when He comes back.

I remember when a boy they used to sing in the Sunday School:

> I think when I read that sweet story of old,
> When Jesus was here among men,
> How He called little children as lambs to His fold.,
> I should like to have been with them then.
>
> I wish that His hands had been placed on my head,
> That His arms had been thrown around me,
> And that I might have seen His kind look when He said,
> 'Let the little ones come unto Me.'

I can remember as well as though it were yesterday how I would say to myself, "My! I wish I had been born eighteen hundred or more years sooner. I wish I had lived when Jesus was here. Those boys in Galilee and Judea had something I will never have. He is so changed now, I will never hear His voice as they did; I will never see those kind eyes as they did; I have been born altogether too late." But after I was saved and began to understand this blessed Book of God, I learned that the same precious, adorable Savior, unchanged and unchangeable, is the One I shall see when He returns. The only difference is that He will come in His kingly robes. He was here on earth in lowly garb, but it is just the outward semblance that is changed. He will be in royal apparel when He returns. How gladly we will greet Him and bow at His feet when we adore Him as King of kings and Lord of lords.

I am wondering if any of you has never trusted this wonderful Savior. He came the first time to put away sin by the sacrifice of Himself and on yonder cross He, the Lord of glory, died. There He bore the judgment that your sins and mine deserved; there as our Surety He took our place. "He was wounded for our transgressions, he was bruised for our iniquities: the chastisement of our peace was upon him; and with his stripes we are healed" (Isaiah 53:5). Today He lives in glory, the exalted One, mighty to save, for "God hath made that same Jesus whom ye crucified," Peter said, "to be both Lord and Christ." And He is the risen One. He is inviting sinners to come to Him, inviting weary burdened souls to find rest at His feet.

> Millions have fled to His spear-pierced side,
> Welcomed they all have been, none were denied.

If I am speaking to one soul who has never trusted in Him, it is not yet too late; you may come now and may know Him as your own personal Savior.

I close by repeating three stanzas of Madge Rae's poem "This Same Jesus."

> 'This same Jesus,' not another,
>   Not a stranger never known,
> But the One who went to Calvary,
>   Died to make me all His own.
> Nineteen hundred years in glory
>   Have not changed Him in the least.
> He, the same who raised a Lazarus,
>   Deigned to sit at Martha's feast!

He it is who cleansed the leper,
  Healed the sick and raised the dead,
Stilled the raging storm-tossed billows,
  And the hungry thousands fed.
HE—I met Him first at Calvary,
  Saw Him standing in my place,
Dying there for me the sinner,
  Oh what matchless, sovereign grace!

May I earthly things hold loosely,
  Counting all but dross for Him,
With my eyes beholding Jesus,
  All beside grows faint and dim.
He is coming, 'this same Jesus';
  Sweet the thought that soon the day,
With its beams of light shall banish
  Earth's dark shadows far away.

Chapter Two

Ungodly Sinners Justified

Now to him that worketh is the reward not reckoned of grace, but of debt. But to him that worketh not, but believeth on him that justifieth the ungodly, his faith is counted for righteousness.

(ROMANS 4: 4-5)

I want to emphasize the central words of that fifth verse, "him that justifieth the ungodly." "Him"—that refers, of course, to God Himself, God the infinitely righteous One, the Holy One. Yet we are told that this righteous God, this holy God, justifies ungodly sinners! This is surely an amazing statement. Can it possibly be true? What is it to justify? It is to pronounce one to be righteous. According to some theologies, justification is said to be that act of God whereby He makes a sinner righteous. But that is clearly a mistake. In justification God is not making the sinner righteous. He does that in sanctification, but justification is a forensic act of God in which He declares a sinner to be righteous.

In the book of the prophet Isaiah we have a very solemn woe pronounced upon those who justify the wicked. It is a very wrong thing for a judge to justify a wicked person, and we have had many complaints in our great cities because public enemies, racketeers, and hoodlums of all kinds have been arrested, and when they have come before corrupt judges, they have been allowed to go free and to prey once more upon the community. People are rightly indignant about it. It is a thoroughly wicked thing for a judge to declare a criminal righteous, yet the singular thing is that this text tells us that it is the very thing God does! God justifies—not the righteous, not good people, not holy people, but the ungodly. How can this be?

What is it to be ungodly? The word really means those who are not pious, not godlike, and that is true of all men by nature. I do not know of any unsaved man who is godly. I have never met an unconverted person that was truly pious, and an ungodly man is one who is unlike God, impious, yet Scripture says that God justifies the ungodly. Whatever does it mean? There is no other religion that teaches anything like this. I am somewhat conversant with practically every well-known religious system in the world. I have been studying these things almost exclusively for over forty years, and I think I can say without boasting that I know pretty well what they all teach in regard to the justification of mankind. I do not know one of them that does not tell men they must produce some kind of a righteousness in order to suit God, before they can ever be justified or accepted of Him. The Christian message stands alone in this respect, for it tells us that God justifies the ungodly. That is one reason why I am absolutely certain this Book is inspired of God. Man would never have thought out anything of the kind. It would never have occurred to him that a holy God, a righteous God, might justify the ungodly. He would take it for granted that before God could justify a man he must do something to deserve that justification, but the sad thing is that nobody can do anything to deserve it.

Have you ever read the Epistle to the Romans carefully? If not, I wish you would begin today and read it right through. It is the most closely reasoned, logical presentation of God's dealings with sinful men that has ever been penned. I look sometimes on the shelves of my own library, and I suppose I have dozens and scores of books written on this little book of sixteen chapters, and then when I have gone through them all, I can ransack the libraries of my friends and find hundreds more. I have often thought, "What a marvelous Book it is that could inspire so many writers." And these few with which I have come in contact are just a fraction of the many books that have been written by some of the most learned, the most intellectual and the most spiritual of men. If you have not studied this book, your education has been tremendously neglected. Do not call yourself a cultured person, an educated person, if you are not familiar with the Epistle to the Romans, because it is one of the most important pieces of literature ever produced.

In Romans 1 God is looking down upon this poor world, seeing the condition of mankind, and He finds that all men are living in sin. He looks over the heathen world, looks at men in their ignorance, in their wickedness as they are in idolatrous countries and gives His judgment concerning them. I often meet people who say, "What are you going to do with the heathen?" I am not going to do anything with them! It is not up to me to do anything with the heathen except to get the gospel to them. But people say, "Are they going to be judged when they have never heard of Christ? Are they going to be damned for rejecting Christ when they have never known of Him?" No, they are not going to be judged for rejecting Christ about whom they have never heard, but the first chapter of Romans shows that they are going to be judged for their own sins: and the heathen are sinners, and more than that, they are not living up to the light they have. People sometimes say, "Why, they have beautiful religions of their own and they are all feeling after God. We need only to give them a little encouragement." We have heard a great deal about this in the recent Laymen's Commission, which is composed of unconverted professors who have been going over mission fields and making what they call an investigation of missions, and they have decided that it is an impertinence for Christian people to go to pagans and give them the gospel.

A young and immature student had just been graduated from the theological seminary. Although I am a teacher in one for a part of the year, yet I can say that very often a theological seminary is a place where young men learn how not to preach! Take a young man who is on fire for God, and if you want to spoil him so that he won't know how or what to preach, send him to a modernist theological seminary and he will be so filled with pride and conceit and a little smattering of Greek, and Hebrew, and "foolosophy" that he will never be able to preach the gospel, until he unlearns the rubbish he has been taught. This young fellow had just been graduated from the seminary; he had also been ordained. Spurgeon once said about ordination, "If it is not the Scriptural kind, it is laying empty hands on an empty head." It doesn't amount to anything. This young man was going out as a missionary. He was giving his valedictory address, and said, "I am not going to tell the heathen that I have a better message than they have; I am not going to give them a gospel that they do not know anything about; but I am going to take my heathen brother by the hand and say, 'Come with me, my brother, we will go together on a quest for God.'" Just imagine a man like that being sent out as a Christian missionary! No gospel to preach! No Christ to proclaim! He had far better stay at home.

According to Romans 1 the heathen are not on a quest for God. We read in Romans 3:11, "There is none that seeketh after God." The heathen have turned away from what they did know of God. Why? Because it made them uncomfortable in their sins. You who are out of Christ know what that means. You were brought up perhaps in Christian homes and have come to this great godless city and have gotten away from righteousness and decency and goodness and purity, and have launched out into the world. You think you are seeing life when in reality you are simply tasting death. You know how you have to try to forget what that godly mother used to teach you, what that Christian father once taught you. You know you do not like to retain these things in your knowledge; you wish you could forget that you ever knelt at a praying mother's knee, that you were ever taught the Bible. Then you think you could sin with impunity.

There was a time when the heathen knew a great deal better than they do now, but they did not like to retain God in their knowledge, so turned away to worship images of all kinds, and even stooped so low as to worship beasts and creeping things. Three times we read in Romans 1, "For this cause God gave them up." "Wherefore God also gave them up to uncleanness through the lusts of their own hearts" (Romans 1:24). "For this cause God gave them up unto vile affections" (Romans 1:26). I cannot read the rest of it in an audience like this. You say, "What, so you think there are things in the Bible too nasty to read in public?" Yes, because they are depicting the sins that men and women commit, and commit with impunity, and those things are in every ungodly person's heart. Read it alone in the presence of God and let Him speak to you through these passages and show you what the human heart is capable of, things that men and women do today unblushingly. Those things that Christless college professors now call Behaviorism; simply letting nature have its way, God declares to be the lust of uncleanness, and men are going to be damned for these things. That is why the heathen are to be judged; that is why they are lost without Christ.

In Romans 1:28 we read, "And even as they did not like to retain God in their knowledge, God gave them over to a reprobate mind, to do those things which are not convenient." The apostle shows the terrible sins they are guilty of, because they have turned from the light they once had. These are the heathen, and they are lost, and people in Christendom are doing the same things and they too are lost. All alike need a Savior. None can save themselves.

Turn to Romans 2 and you will find that in the first part you have another class, a cultured, educated group such as the philosophers, who prided themselves upon their knowledge and gloried in not being so low and vulgar and degraded as the more ignorant heathen. They sat in judgment on others, and God says, as it were, "You who judge others, you are doing the same things, only you keep your sins covered up a little more; you are guilty of the same wicked things, only you are not so openly brazen about them, but you are committing them just the same and are therefore just as guilty and subject to the righteous judgment of God." Any one familiar with ancient history knows how terribly true this was.

Then he turns to the third class, a people who had the Bible and had received instruction out of the law of God, the Jews. They had the Old Testament, they prided themselves on belonging to God's covenant people. To them, He says, "Very well, you are called a Jew and rest in the law and make your boast of God and know His will and profess to approve the things that are excellent; are you any better in heart, are you purer in your life than your Gentile neighbor?" Not a bit. He declares, "The name of God is blasphemed among the Gentiles through you" (Romans 2:24). They looked at the Jew and said, "He professes to have the true God and yet he lives just like the rest of us." That is what they are saying about a lot of professing Christians today. "They belong to the church, they have been baptized, they partake of the sacrament, but they are just like the rest of us."

A gentleman told me one day that he went to a certain church and they were going to have the Lord's Supper. He got up to move away, for he did not feel that he ought to partake. Just then he noticed a business associate of his, who leaned over and put his hand on his shoulder and said, "Just take it with the rest of us. We are all a lot of hypocrites anyway." And he drank of that cup and ate of that bread! What a shame that people are forever covering up, covering up, covering up, and yet know in their own hearts that they are guilty before God; "eating and drinking judgment to themselves."

Paul concludes this review of all mankind in Romans 3, and says, "There is none righteous, no, not one." They are all under sin. How many righteous? Not one. Not even you? No. Not even me? Oh, no, I found that out long ago about myself. "There is none righteous, no, not one. . . . There is none that doeth good, no, not [so much as] one" (Romans 3:10-12). What a wretched condition we are in. Nobody but righteous and good people will ever be in Heaven and here is a world filled with unrighteous and ungodly sinners! We cannot help ourselves, we cannot cleanse our own hearts, we cannot make ourselves any better, try and struggle as we may. We cannot purify that cesspool of iniquity in our breasts. "Out of the heart proceed evil thoughts, fornication, and adultery." These could not come out of the heart if they were not there beforehand. But what are we going to do about it? God says, "The thing for you to learn is that you cannot do anything."

> Could my zeal no respite know,
> Could my tears forever flow,
> All for sin could not atone;
> Thou must save, and Thou alone.
> (Augustus M. Toplady)

The next part of the Epistle to the Romans opens that up to us. In Romans 3:21 we read, "But now"—"now" is an adverb of time. When? After he has proven that all have sinned, that all are ungodly, that all are unrighteous, that there is none that doeth good, "now the righteousness of God without the law is manifested." God has a righteousness for unrighteous sinners who have nothing of goodness to plead. And what is this righteousness of God? God looked in pity upon men in their sins and iniquity, His holy nature demanded that sin be dealt with, so He came down into this world in the person of His own blessed Son, and there on Calvary's cross drank to the very depths the cup of judgment that our sins deserved. Think of it! The Lord Jesus, the holy One, the just One, suffered on Calvary's cross that which your sins and my sins deserved, as though He had been as corrupt, wicked, licentious, untruthful, unholy, and unchaste as men and women in this world are today. He who is absolutely pure and undefiled, drank to the depths the cup of judgment.

> His the wormwood and the gall,
> His the curse, He bore them all;
> His the bitter cry of pain
> When our sins He did sustain.

This explains that cry from Calvary, "My God, my God, why hast thou forsaken me?" It was because you and I deserved to be forsaken, because you and I were so utterly unfit for God that He could do nothing but turn His face from us. He was of purer eyes than to behold iniquity and so God "made him to be sin for us, who knew no sin; that we might be made the righteousness of God in him" (2 Corinthians 5:21). God had to act in consistency with His own character before He could offer a righteous salvation to any one. He did this on the cross.

He has set Christ forth a Prince and a Savior. He died for our sins; He has been raised from the dead for our justification, and now God comes to guilty men and women and says, "You need no longer be debarred from Heaven because of your sins, I have provided a ransom; I have a Deliverer for you, and if you will put your trust in my blessed Son, take Him as your Savior, give up all pretension of righteousness, come to Him just as you are, I stand ready to justify the ungodly."

But somebody says, "I would like to come to a God like that, who is so good and so gracious, but I do not feel good enough." You are barking up the wrong tree. It is not a question of being good enough; the question is, are you bad enough? When He was here on earth, the Pharisees derided Him and said, "This man receiveth sinners, and eateth with them" (Luke 15:2), but He said, "I am not come to call the righteous, but sinners to repentance" (Matthew 9:13). If there is a man or woman who can prove that he has never sinned, I can prove from this Book that there is no Savior for him. There is no Savior for righteous people, for good people, but Christ is the Savior of sinners. "They that are whole need not a physician; but they that are sick" (Luke 5:31).

A young man who often listened to a great Scotch preacher wanted to be saved. He had a great longing in his heart to know Christ as his Deliverer, to know the blessedness of God's salvation, and although he wept and prayed and sought, he could get no sense of forgiveness, no assurance that he was received by God. One night the minister preached on those words, "I am the door: by me if any man enter in, he shall be saved" (John 10:9), and he showed that "any man" took in poor sinners, no matter how vile, how wicked, how corrupt they were. As he preached, he could see the cloud lift from this young man's face, and at the close of the meeting he came to the front and said, "I got in tonight."

"What do you mean?" asked the preacher.

"Why, I got in at the open door tonight while you were preaching."

"I am glad to hear it. But why did you not get in before? You have been troubled for a fortnight and I have been trying to help you, and others have been doing their best to help you. How was it that you did not get in until tonight?"

"Well," said the young man, "I have been at the wrong door all the time. I have been knocking at the saint's door and I found it locked against me. I thought I had to become good enough for God to save me, but I said tonight, I will try the sinner's door, and when I came to it, it was open and I got right inside."

A great many people are not saved because they will not take the place of a lost sinner; they will never bow low enough.

There is a story told of an old man who owned a little narrow lot, with a poor miserable cabin on it. Lots in his neighborhood had been selling for fabulous prices and he felt that some day his place would make his fortune. By and by a millionaire came along and seeing the possibilities of that block, said, "I want the whole thing." He sent his agent to go and buy up the block, and when he came to the old man, he said, "What would you sell your place for?" He had waited long for this opportunity and so he put up what he thought was a tremendous big figure. "Very well," said the agent, "I will take it." "When do you want it?" the old man asked. "In about two weeks I will be around with the deed and you can be ready to sign it. Here is a thousand dollars to bind the sale," replied the agent. The old man was simply delighted and thought, "Well, if somebody has bought this place who is able to pay all that money, I ought to fix it up a bit." And so he bought some paint and went to work painting the old place. He bought some glass to replace the broken panes, and for two weeks he worked on the cabin. When this millionaire purchaser and his agent brought the papers for him to sign, he was so nervous about it he could hardly hold the pen. He was surprised that the purchaser did not say anything about the shack and so he said, "You see how beautifully I have painted it up and have put in some new windows. It is going to make a nice place. I hope you will be very comfortable in it." "Oh," said the millionaire, "but I didn't buy this place for what is on it, but for what I am going to put on it." That is how God justifies the ungodly. It is not because of what He finds in men, but He saves them for what He is going to put in them, for what He is going to do for them. When they put their trust in Him, they get everlasting life, they are justified, and all their sins are forgiven. Then God proceeds to make them fit for His own blessed presence, and when we get home to Heaven, we will give Him all the glory.

Have you trusted Him? He justifies the ungodly. Are you ungodly? He is waiting to justify you. "Be it known unto you therefore, men and brethren, that through this man is preached unto you the forgiveness of sins; and by him all that believe are justified from all things, from which ye could not be justified by the law of Moses" (Acts 13:38-39).

> He tells me words whereby I'm saved,
>   He points to something DONE,
> Accomplished on Mount Calvary,
>   By His beloved Son;
> In which no works of mine have place,
> Else grace with works is no more grace.
>
> Believing this, how can I wait,
>   And ask what shall I DO
> To make His gift more sure to me;
>   His loving words more true?
> Since works of mine have here no place,
> Else grace with works is no more grace.
>
> Ah, no; it is His FINISHED work
>   On which my soul relies;
> And if my unbelieving heart
>   Its preciousness denies,
> That works of mine might have a place;
> Then grace with works is no more grace.

Chapter Three

Saved By His Life

For if, when we were enemies, we were reconciled to God by the death of his Son, much more, being reconciled, we shall be saved by his life.
(Romans 5:10)

It is not the entire verse I am thinking of today so much as the last four words, "*Saved by his life.*" What are we to understand by this expression? Certainly the verse itself and the entire context makes it very plain that it is through the death of Christ our sins are put away. It is His precious atoning blood that cleanses us from all sin, thus purging our guilty consciences. It is through the work of His cross that we have peace with God; and yet here the apostle declares, "We shall be saved by his life."

Let us first consider what these words do not mean. "Saved by his life" does not imply that salvation comes through seeking to imitate the beautiful holy life of our blessed Lord. Let me say it seriously, earnestly, following Jesus will not save any one! Often the Christless are earnestly exhorted to begin the Christian life by taking up their cross and endeavoring to follow Jesus in order that they might be saved. But this is a travesty of the gospel. No one was ever saved by imitating the life of Jesus or attempting to do so. His life was an absolutely holy life. There was not one thought or act that did not have the Father's approbation. He said with truth, "I do always those things which please him." And the Father Himself declared, "This is my beloved Son in whom I am well pleased." If salvation comes through imitating Him in His holy ways here on earth, then you and I are as good as lost eternally even now. For it is utterly impossible for a sinful man or woman to follow in the steps of the sinless Savior. And yet the apostle Peter tells us, He hath "left us an example that [we] should follow his steps." But he is speaking to Christians, not to those who are seeking salvation. We who are saved are now born again and indwelt by the Holy Spirit. With His gracious aid we are enabled at least in some measure to imitate the example of our blessed Savior. But the holiest Christian would be the last man on earth to insist that he was saved by following in the steps of Jesus.

Then again "saved by his life" does not mean that we are saved through the wonderful life that our Lord lived, as though that life were acceptable as an atonement for our sinful, evil lives. The life of the Lord Jesus on earth apart from His death would never have saved one poor sinner. He came into the world for the express purpose of laying down His life a ransom for many. As the God-appointed Paschal Lamb, He must be the unblemished One. His holy and righteous life proved Him to be the fit substitute for sinful men. But that life had to be given up in death before our guilt could be atoned for and our iniquities blotted out. The natural heart rebels at the doctrine of the blood, but the Bible bears consistent witness from the offering of Abel's lamb at the gate of Eden to the song of the redeemed in the Book of Revelation, that salvation is not by the life of Jesus, but by the shedding of His precious blood. This comes out in vivid contrast, if we consider the well-known words of the founder of a very popular religious system today. She has written: "The material blood of Jesus was no more able to cleanse from sin when it was shed upon the accursed tree than when it was flowing in His veins as He went about daily doing His Father's business." But our Savior Himself, when He instituted the last supper said, as He gave the cup to His disciples, "This is my blood of the new testament, which is shed for many for the remission of sins" (Matthew 26:28). It is impossible to reconcile these two statements. The one denies the cleansing efficacy of the shed blood. The other declares the blood was shed for the express purpose of the remission of sins. Whatever "saved by his life," means, it cannot then mean that it is His life on earth rather than His death that makes it possible for guilty sinners to be justified by a holy God.

Before attempting to show what the words actually do mean, let me point out what to many will be familiar truth already. Salvation is presented in the New Testament in a threefold way: All who believe in the Lord Jesus Christ are saved from the guilt of sin and from the judgment due to sin. This salvation is complete and eternal from the moment we believe. To it the apostle refers when he says, "By grace are ye saved through faith; and that not of yourselves; it is the gift of God; Not of works, lest any man should boast." And again he tells us, "Not by works of righteousness which we have done, but according to his mercy he saved us, by the washing of regeneration, and renewing of the Holy Ghost." Many other passages emphasize the same wondrous fact that we are already saved if we have put our trust in the Lord Jesus Christ.

But this is not all there is to salvation. Having been saved from the guilt of sin we who are Christians are now being saved daily, hourly, momentarily from the power of sin through the intercession of the risen Christ, and the work of the indwelling Holy Spirit. By and by when we are gathered home with the Lord, we shall be saved from the presence of sin, when we are fully conformed to the image of God's beloved Son. Now it is to these second and third aspects of salvation that the words of the text apply. We who have already been reconciled to God by the death of His Son shall be saved by His life. That is, His resurrection life. He who died for us on the cross to settle the sin question, now lives in glory to complete in us the work which

His grace has begun. It is as the risen One, He says, "Because I live, ye shall live also."

It is right here that many need help. Often in speaking with exercised souls urging immediate trust in Christ and confession of Him as Savior, one is met by the anxious reply, "I would like to come to Christ but I am afraid I can never hold out. I might become a Christian today and afterwards bring such disgrace on the name of the Lord by lapsing into sin that I am afraid to venture. It is not that I do not trust Christ, but the fact is I do not trust myself. I know my own propensities and proclivities so well; I am so conscious of sinful habits that dominate and control my life that even though intellectually convinced that Jesus is the only Savior, I do not dare trust myself to Him and confess Him openly for fear I could not hold out. I feel it would be better never to have made a profession than to disgrace it all by failure afterwards."

My dear troubled one, let me now seek as God by His Spirit will enable, to bring before you the encouragement that lies in the four words of my brief text. We are "saved by his life." You are not asked to trust Christ in order that your sins up to the time of your conversion may be put away, and then that you should be left on your own resources to do your best to live a Christian life with possibly failure in prospect eventually, but the Spirit of God would have you see that He who loved you enough to die for you on the cross, now lives to sustain and maintain all who believe in Him, in order that they may walk as He walked and glorify God in their daily lives. He is not less interested in us after having died for us, but now in Heaven He is daily saving His people from their sins, keeping them by His mighty power. In the Epistle to the Hebrews, we read, "Wherefore he is able also to save them to the uttermost that come unto God by him, seeing he ever liveth to make intercession for them." What a glorious truth is here revealed! As our High Priest with God, He ever gives us a perfect representation before the throne of God in Heaven. He makes constant intercession for us presenting His own excellencies on our behalf. And He sits there enthroned as a reservoir of all that we need for our pilgrim path, bidding us come boldly to a throne of grace, that we may obtain mercy and find grace for seasonable help. All that we need in the conflict with sin to enable us to come out victoriously, He waits to supply. We have only to draw by faith upon His infinite resources. But more than this, by the Spirit He now indwells all believers. "If any man have not the Spirit of Christ he is none of his." The indwelling Spirit is the Spirit of power and of holiness, and as we walk in the Spirit we are definitely promised that we shall not fulfill the lusts of the flesh.

"Ah," exclaims some one, "I begin to see now, I think, what it means to be saved by His life. But even though there are infinite resources in Christ of which I may avail myself, is there not still danger that I may fail to do this and hence may break down completely after all, and so my last end be worse than the beginning?"

Unquestionably we are all liable to failure. But let us remember that failure does not involve separation from Christ. In respect to this also, we shall be saved by His life, for it is written, "My little children, these things write I unto you that ye sin not, and if any man sin, we have an advocate with the Father, Jesus Christ the righteous; And he is the propitiation for our sins, and not for ours only, but also for the sins of the whole world" (1 John 2:1-2). Christians are not perfect people. We still have within us the old nature though we have been born again. The Lord Jesus says, "That which is born of the flesh is flesh, and that which is born of the Spirit is spirit." No amount of Christian nurture will change flesh into spirit. "The carnal mind is not subject to the law of God, neither indeed can be." If we are looking for improvement in ourselves after conversion, we shall be disappointed. We need to recognize that in us, that is, in our flesh, dwells no good thing. The Word of God like a mirror exposes us to ourselves. It tells us what the works of the flesh are, and against these we need to be continually on our guard.

I ran across an illustration the other day that I think pictures this admirably. An elderly gentleman who was very nearsighted prided himself on his ability as an art critic. On one occasion he was accompanying some friends through a large gallery and was seeking to display his real or fancied knowledge of pictures to them. He had left his glasses at home and was not able to see things very clearly. Standing before a large frame, he began to point out the inartistic features of the picture there revealed. "The frame," he said, "is altogether out of keeping with the subject, and as for the subject itself (it was that of a man), it is altogether too homely, in fact too ugly, ever to make a good picture. It is a great mistake for any artist to choose so homely a subject for a picture if he expects it to be a masterpiece." The old gentleman was going on like this when his wife managed to get near enough to interrupt. She exclaimed, "My dear, you are looking into a mirror," and he was quite taken aback to realize that he had been criticizing his own face.

Now the Word of God is such a mirror. It does not hide our deformities. It shows us up just as we are. But we are not to be occupied with our old selves. The Spirit of God would turn us away from self altogether to occupation with the risen Christ, and as we are taken up with Him, we are kept from sin. It is when we get our eyes off Christ and become self-occupied or taken up with the world around us that we fail. And who of us does not so fail? We all have to confess our failures from day to day, but our ever-living Savior is not only our High Priest to minister all needed grace and help, but even when we fail to avail ourselves of that as we should, He is our Advocate still, and the moment we fail He takes up our case with the Father.

Mark, it does not say, "If any man confess his sin, we have an advocate," but rather, "If any man sin, we have an advocate." The moment we fail He is in the Father's presence about us, and as a result of His gracious advocacy, the Spirit continues His work in our hearts bringing us to repentance and confession, and, "If we confess our sins he is faithful and just to forgive us our sins, and to cleanse us from all unrighteousness." And so "we shall be saved by his life."

Then when at last our time of toiling and fighting here on earth shall come to an end and our Lord shall receive us to Himself, He, the ever-living One, will save us completely from the very presence of sin so that we shall never be so much as tempted again for all eternity, but will be preserved inviolate in holiness before the face of God our Father. Thus in the fullest possible sense we shall be forever "saved by his life."

What encouragement then this should give to the anxious trembling sinner who is alarmed as he thinks of judgment ahead; he yearns for forgiveness and justification but he fears he will never be able to glorify God in his life afterward. The same One who loved you enough to die for you and now bids you trust Him as your Savior, is the One who lives in the glory to guide us, and has declared, His sheep "shall never perish." Trust Him then, I beseech you, today, and having been reconciled to God by the death of His Son, you will know the blessedness of being "saved by his life."

Chapter Four

The Sacrifice Bound to the Altar

A Communion Meditation

Bind the sacrifice with cords, even unto the horns of the altar.
(Psalm 118:27)

You will readily recognize the reference to the altar of burnt offering which of old stood just inside the gate of the tabernacle. It was made of acacia wood overlaid with brass or copper, and had a grate in the center of it where the victim was burned, typifying the atoning work of our Lord Jesus Christ. As these various sacrificial beasts were brought to be offered to Jehovah, they were bound to the horns of the altar, which were upon its four corners.

In this Scripture, which is a Messianic Psalm, picturing our Lord Jesus Christ as the rejected One giving Himself for us, we see the meaning of the horns. He was bound to them. It is in this same Psalm that we read, "The stone which the builders refused is become the head stone of the corner." It speaks of our Lord Jesus, the One who "came to his own, but his own received him not." He was rejected by those He loved so tenderly and was taken out to die. He was the victim bound as it were to the horns of the altar. That altar for Him was the cross on which He yielded up His life for our redemption. The horn signifies power—the gospel is the power of God unto salvation to all who believe. Four speaks of universality—He gave Himself a ransom for all.

What were the cords that bound Him there? It is a rather significant thing that the only other instance in all the Bible, as far as I can recall, where we actually read of a sacrifice being bound to the altar is in the case of Isaac. God said to Abraham, "Take now thy son, thine only son Isaac, whom thou lovest, and get thee into the land of Moriah; and offer him there for a burnt offering upon one of the mountains which I will tell thee of." And we are told how the father and son went together to mount Moriah, and how Isaac looked up to his father and said, "Behold the fire and the wood: but where is the lamb for the burnt offering?" Abraham replied, "My son, God will provide himself a lamb for a burnt offering." What prophetic words were those! Jesus said, "Abraham rejoiced to see my day." He looked on in faith to the coming into this scene of "the Lamb of God which taketh away the sin of the world." But again typically we read, "Abraham built an altar there, and laid the wood in order, and bound Isaac his son, and laid him on the altar upon the wood. And Abraham stretched forth his hand, and took the knife to slay his son." Then God intervened. Someone has well said, "He spared that father's heart the pang which He would not spare His own." This is the fullest picture of the sacrifice of Christ which we have in the Old Testament. Elsewhere we read of bulls and goats and rams offered to God, but here we have a man; here we have a beloved son bound with cords to the altar.

What were the cords? It seems to me we might think of one of them as "The Golden Cord of Love to God the Father." You remember how our Lord Jesus Christ declared in John's Gospel, "No man taketh [My life] from me, but I lay it down of myself. I have power to lay it down, and I have power to take it again. This commandment have I received of my Father" (John 10:18). And again you recall His words, as He left the upper room to go out to the garden, "That the world may know that I love the Father; and as the Father gave me commandment, even so I do. Arise, let us go hence" (John 14:31). He was not a helpless victim in the hands of wicked men. He had demonstrated over and over again that they had no real power over Him. Three years before when He preached that wonderful sermon in the synagogue of Nazareth they led Him out of the city and were determined to hurl Him over the cliff and dash Him to pieces on the rocks below; but, "He passing through the midst of them went his way" (Luke 4:30). Not one hand was raised to detain Him. They came to Him in the garden on the night of His sorrows, as He prayed, "O my Father, if it be possible, let this cup pass from me: nevertheless not as I will, but as thou wilt" (Matthew 26:39). And when at last He saw the multitude coming He went forth to meet them and asked, "Whom seek ye?" And they said, "We seek Jesus of Nazareth." And He answered, "I am he." In so speaking He used the incommunicable name of God. Moses said to Jehovah, "When I come to the children of Israel, whom shall I say sent me?" God's answer was, "I AM; say unto the children of Israel, I AM hath sent me unto you." When they came with swords and staves to arrest Jesus, He said, "I am," and they went backward and fell to the ground. They could not stand before His face when He asserted His Deity. They had no power against Him. He had insisted upon that when He stood in Pilate's Hall. Pilate asked Him, "Speakest thou not unto me? knowest thou not that I have power to crucify thee and have power to release thee?" Jesus replied, "Thou couldest have no power at all against me, except it were given thee from above" (John 19:11). So He put Himself in their hands and went out to die voluntarily, and the Sacrifice was bound to the horns of the altar. What was the cord that bound Him there? "But that the world may know that I love the Father; and as the Father gave me commandment, even so I do. Arise, let us go hence."

It was love to the Father; it was the desire to vindicate the righteousness of God; it was that He might glorify the Father, that led Him thus to go to that cross.

But that is only one of the cords that bound Him. The text intimates that there were more than one. "Bind the sacrifice with cords, even unto the horns of the altar." We may speak of the other as, "The Silver Cord of Love to Man," for in Ephesians 5:25-26 it is written, "Christ loved the church, and gave himself for it; That he might sanctify and cleanse it with the washing of water by the word." He could have gone free. The law had no claim upon Him. Jehovah had decreed, "The soul that sinneth it shall die;" but He had never been guilty of sin, He was free from all inward tendency to sin, and yet He stooped in grace to take our place and went out to die in our room and stead. Never was love like His. You remember He said, "Greater love hath no man than this, that a man lay down his life for his friends." It was in grace He called them friends, for by nature all men are enemies and alienated from God by wicked works. If He had been looking for friends for whom to die, He could not have found one in all this wide world, for of every man's heart it is written, "The carnal mind is enmity against God" (Romans 8:7). It is His love that makes us His friends. He looked on to what His grace would accomplish and He saw us as we would be when responsive to His mercy and lovingkindness, and so treated us as friends and went to the cross to die for His friends. "Bind the sacrifice with cords, even to the horns of the altar"—the golden cord of love for God, because He was there to fulfill God's righteousness, and gold is the symbol of divine righteousness in Scripture; the silver cord of love to man, for He was there to procure our redemption and salvation, and silver is the symbol of redemption in the Book of God.

> 'Twas love that sought Gethsemane,
>   Or Judas ne'er had found Him;

> 'Twas love that held Him to the tree,
> Or iron ne'er had bound Him.

What is our responsibility to love like this? Is it enough that putting our trust in Him as Savior we shall know that He has put our sins away and fitted us for the presence of God? Shall we stop there? Is it enough that we come together from time to time and look back by faith to that cross and contemplate that love, meditate upon that mighty sacrifice with our hearts going out in worship and praise and adoration? Shall we stop there? Or shall we remember that love like this has claims on us and that as He was bound to the horns of the altar, so now the word comes home to every redeemed soul: "I beseech you therefore, brethren, by the mercies of God, that ye present your bodies a living sacrifice, holy, acceptable unto God, which is your reasonable service" (Romans 12:1). Shall we not turn to Him and say, "Blessed Lord, Thou wert bound with cords to the horns of the altar in order to redeem our souls from everlasting judgment. Oh, bind us to the place of sacrifice that we may be yielded wholly to Thyself, that we may live unto Thee. Now bind us there that we may not shrink back, but ever offer to Thee the sacrifice of praise and thanksgiving, and the sacrifice of well-doing to glorify Thy name."

The early Christians used to speak of the Lord's Supper as "The Sacrament." Sometimes we lose track of the origin of these ecclesiastical terms and we wonder at them. How would anybody ever think of calling the eucharistic feast a *Sacrament*? This was the name given to the oath taken by a Roman legionary when he enlisted in the Imperial army. He took the oath of fealty to the emperor, of loyalty to Rome, of devotion to those in authority above him; and from time to time as the troops were reviewed and they saluted the emperor, this oath was renewed. So the early Christians came to think of each observance of the Lord's Supper as a renewal of their allegiance to the Savior who had bought them with His blood and was now their risen Lord. Thus, little by little, they came to regard it as a sacramental service.

Perhaps the term has been misused. I am afraid it has. We have lost sight of the simplicity of the feast of remembrance. Traditional teaching has superseded the clear instruction of the Holy Scriptures. Ritualistic and liturgical practices have obscured the true character of the Supper of the Lord. But nevertheless we can well understand the thought that was in the minds of those early believers when they spoke of it as they did, and surely all who draw near to the Lord's table should know what it is to realize afresh their eternal obligation to Him who has bought us with His own most precious blood. As we meet in hallowed communion to remember Him who remembered us in our great need, we may well look back and think of Him as the one all-sufficient sacrifice for sin bound by the cords of love to the horns of the altar. And as we partake of the bread and the cup should we not lift our hearts afresh and say, "Blessed Lord, Thou hast died so great a death for me, Thou hast manifested such a marvelous love in the accomplishment of my redemption; now, anew, I yield myself unreservedly to Thee to be for Thy glory and praise while I am left in this scene."

To any who are still strangers to the matchless grace of God revealed in Christ, I beseech you, in lowliness of mind and with reverent mien draw near and see this great sight—the sinless Savior bound to the altar for sinful men! Bow in penitence at His pierced feet and trust Him now as your very own Redeemer and confess Him as your Lord.

> My Redeemer! O what beauties,
> In that lovely name appear;
> None but Jesus in His glories
> Shall the honored title wear.
> My Redeemer! O, how sweet
> To call Thee mine!

Chapter Five

The Message of Pentecost

Ye men of Israel, hear these words; Jesus of Nazareth, a man approved of God among you by miracles and wonders and signs, which God did by him in the midst of you, as ye yourselves also know: Him, being delivered by the determinate counsel and foreknowledge of God, ye have taken, and by wicked hands have crucified and slain; Whom God hath raised up, having loosed the pains of death; because it was not possible that he should be holden of it. For David speaketh concerning him, I foresaw the Lord always before my face; for he is on my right hand, that I should not be moved; Therefore did my heart rejoice, and my tongue was glad: moreover also my flesh shall rest in hope; Because thou wilt not leave my soul in hell, neither wilt thou suffer thine Holy One to see corruption. Thou hast made me full of joy with thy countenance. Men and brethren, let me freely speak unto you of the patriarch David, that he is both dead and buried, and his sepulchre is with us unto this day. Therefore being a prophet, and knowing that God had sworn with an oath to him, that of the fruit of his loins, according to the flesh, he would raise up Christ to sit on his throne; He seeing this before spake of the resurrection of Christ, that his soul was not left in hell, neither his flesh did see corruption. This Jesus hath God raised up, whereof we all are witnesses. Therefore being by the right hand of God exalted, and having received of the Father the promise of the Holy Ghost, he hath shed forth this, which ye now see and hear. For David is not ascended into the heavens; but he said himself, The Lord said unto my Lord, Sit thou on my right hand, until I make thy foes thy footstool. Therefore let all the house of Israel know assuredly, that God hath made that same Jesus, whom ye have crucified, both Lord and Christ.
(Acts 2:22-36)

I want you to look with me at a sermon that another man preached over nineteen hundred years ago; a sermon that had greater results probably than any other that has ever been preached in the history of the world.

You all know, of course, that it is a little over nineteen hundred years since the Holy Spirit came on that wondrous Pentecost at Jerusalem. Our chronology is reasonably certain excepting that when the calendar was arranged as we have it now, those who had charge of these matters were misled on account of a misunderstanding of the Roman calendar. We say B.C., before Christ, and A.D., Anno Domini, since Christ, the year of our Lord. Somebody has said, "His pierced hand lifted empires off their hinges and changed the course of ages." We date everything from the time that Christ Jesus came into the world. Chronologists discovered a few hundred years ago that those who had computed those dates had been misled in some particulars, and that our Lord Jesus was born four years earlier than the supposed date of His birth. He was in this scene thirty-three and one-half years, therefore He was crucified in all probability in the spring of A.D. 30, although some think it was more likely in A.D. 29. Fifty days after His resurrection the Holy Spirit came at Pentecost. On the morning of that day the twelve apostles came together to wait upon God, and with them a number of others who brought the entire company up to one hundred and twenty. The twelve who had the prominent place were those who had been associated with the Lord Jesus Christ in His life on earth "from the days of John the Baptist, until the day in which he was taken up."

Judas had proven recreant, and after selling his Lord had committed suicide, going "to his own place." Though bearing the name of a disciple, he was ever "a devil." But in place of Judas another had been chosen, Matthias. He had been an eyewitness of the work of the Lord Jesus Christ. These men had been commissioned by the Savior to go out "into all the world, and preach the gospel to every creature." They were largely illiterate. They had had very few advantages, thinking of them from the scholastic standpoint. But as they had been instructed by the greatest teacher who had ever walked this earth, spiritually and intellectually too, they had enjoyed remarkable privileges. They had been transformed by the years of companionship with Him. But there they were, a forlorn little company; they had seen their Lord crucified, they had given up hope; they said, "We thought it was he who should deliver us," but His death seemed to end all that. Then they were electrified to hear that the stone had been rolled away from the door of the tomb, and they thought His enemies had stolen His body. His foes were as perturbed as they, for their greatest desire was that He should remain forever in the tomb.

Suddenly the blessed Lord appeared to His disciples, and in such a way that there could be no doubt that He was the same blessed One who had been nailed to the cross, who had gone through all the agonies of the tree and cried out in His anguish, "My God, my God, why hast thou forsaken me?"

He was risen, no question about it. If His enemies had stolen the body they would have produced it, for they would realize that they had made the greatest possible mistake. If the disciples had taken it they would have produced it, for they were upset to think that their enemies might have taken it. But they had to believe that He had risen when they saw Him. He could actually say to a doubter, "Reach hither thy hand, and thrust it into my side; and be not faithless, but believing" (John 20:27). During forty days the risen Lord gave them a postgraduate course in Christian service and commissioned them to carry His gospel into all the world, and yet those men shrank from the task before them. But He told them not to begin until a new power should come to them. "Tarry ye in the city of Jerusalem, until ye be endued with power from on high" (Luke 24:49). And they waited for ten days after He had ascended to Heaven and then we are told that "when the day of Pentecost was fully come, they were all with one accord in one place. And suddenly there came a sound from heaven as of a rushing mighty wind, and it filled all the house where they were sitting" (Acts 2:1-2). Oh, the solemnity of it! Imagine what it must have meant to them when suddenly they heard that sound from heaven. There was no evidence of storm in the sky and yet there came "a sound from heaven as of a rushing mighty wind, and it filled all the house where they were sitting." Then as they gazed one upon another "there appeared unto them cloven tongues like as of fire, and it sat upon each of them" (Acts 2:3). The Spirit had come in cleansing power and had come to empower them to carry the message of the gospel in the tongues of all men to the very ends of the world. They were to go forth to win men, not with human reason nor by grace nor by their eloquence, but with the tongue of fire, the tongue touched by the Holy Spirit. They were filled with the Holy Spirit and their filling was not just for their own satisfaction; it was not simply for their own joy and gladness; it was not a mere emotional experience that would give them a certain ecstatic sensation; but they were filled in order that they might be the messengers of grace to a dying world, and "they began to speak with other tongues as the Spirit gave them utterance."

Thousands of years before, men rose up in their pride when God had commanded them to scatter on the face of the earth, and undertook to build a tower that would reach to heaven and said, "We will remain here and we will be strong in our own strength, in our own power." But we read that God came down to see the tower which the children of men had built, and He confounded their tongues so that they were not able to understand one another's speech. One man asked for bricks in one language and he was answered in bewilderment by his brother in another language. The work ceased and they were scattered abroad. But on the day of Pentecost the very opposite miracle was wrought. God used men, all of whom were Galileans, to preach in languages that they had never learned, and gave them opportunity to manifest this new power which they had received.

The Jews had come up to Jerusalem from their own countries where they had been scattered, in order to worship God at Pentecost, and there they were all ready for the message. They were amazed to hear every man speak in their own language and they said, "Behold, are not all these which speak Galileans?" Remember, we have no intimation that anyone but the twelve had this marvelous manifestation. It was the twelve apostles who were preaching in tongues that day; not the one hundred and twenty, not the people who were converted afterward. And yet they said, "How hear we every man in our own tongue, wherein we were born? Parthians, and Medes, and Elamites, and the dwellers in Mesopotamia, and in Judea, and Cappadocia, in Pontus, and Asia, Phrygia, and Pamphylia, in Egypt, and in the parts of Libya about Cyrene, and strangers of Rome, Jews and proselytes, Cretes and Arabians,, we do hear them speak in our tongues the wonderful works of God." They could not explain it. "Why," they said, "what meaneth this?" Those who could understand the different languages could get what was being preached; those who did not understand thought the men were just babbling and said, "These men are full of new wine." It was not that they were acting in an erratic manner, but as they preached in these strange languages the Palestine Jews said, "Why, these men are babbling drunkards!" But Peter replied, "No, no; this is the very same power that was spoken of in the book of the prophet Joel." He did not say that this is the fulfillment of the prophet Joel, for when Joel's prophecy will be completely fulfilled there shall appear "wonders in the heavens and in the earth, blood, and fire, and pillars of smoke" (Joel 2:30). But the very same power that is going to work then was the power that was working at Pentecost, and so

Peter said, "This is that which was spoken by the prophet Joel."

The same Spirit, the same power, came at that day to accompany the ministry of the gospel, and in that power Peter preached the Word. Do you wonder as you read it, how it was that it produced such tremendous results? I did not hear any man cry for mercy; I did not hear anyone sobbing over his sins when we read it this morning; but when Peter preached, the effect was electric; it stirred his great audience from the center to the circumference. Those people were all familiar with the events that had just taken place; they knew how Jesus had been denied in Pilate's judgment hall, how He had been crucified, laid in a tomb, and now Peter's solemnly attested declaration is that Jesus, whom many of them had seen carried to the tomb, had been raised in power and was living to save. It stirred those people to the very depths of their being. Oh, that the Spirit who gave power to the message nineteen hundred years ago might give power to it as I read it again to you today.

"Ye men of Israel"—let me change it—You men of Chicago, you who are here today out of Christ, you who are more or less familiar with these things but have never allowed them to grip your heart and conscience, "hear these words; Jesus of Nazareth, a man approved of God among you by miracles and signs, which God did by him in the midst of you, as ye yourselves also know." Jesus came in exact accord with the prophetic Word; everything was headed up in Him. He came in the way of righteousness; He said the things that He had been expected to say, and yet, alas, they rejected Him. People say, "If we could only see miracles wrought; if the ministers today could work signs and wonders, people would believe." Not at all! No one was ever converted to God by a miracle. God has given miracles in order to attest His message. Even if we could call the dead to life, men would no more believe than they do when the gospel is preached.

You remember that rich man who died and went down into Hades, and cried, "I pray thee, therefore . . . that thou wouldest send [Lazarus] to my father's house: For I have five brethren; that he may testify unto them lest they also come into this place of torment" (Luke 16:27-28). Think of it! Six brothers, one in hell and five on the way. What a family! And that man in Hell said, "I do not want my brothers to come here; send Lazarus to them." But Abraham said, "They have Moses and the prophets; let them hear them," let them read their Bible, let them accept the message of the Bible. That rich man knew how he himself had neglected his Bible, and he knew his brethren were just like him, and said, "Nay, father Abraham: but if one went unto them from the dead, they will repent" (Luke 16:30). And Abraham said—Hear it, Christless soul, you who have sometimes said, "If God only gave me some other advantages than those He has given in His Word"—Abraham said, "If they hear not Moses and the prophets, neither will they be persuaded, though one rose from the dead" (Luke 16:31). What does this mean? Just this, that if men will not believe the Bible, they will not believe the greatest possible miracle; they would call it all in question, they would not accept it. Oh, my friend, God is not speaking to you through miracles but He has sent His Word which Jesus attested by miracles. Would men accept Him? They cried, "Away with him! Away with him! Crucify him!"

But now, see how Peter drives that home. "Him, being delivered by the determinate counsel and foreknowledge of God"— nothing took God by surprise. He knew just what they would do, but that does not lessen their sinfulness—"Ye have taken and with wicked hands have crucified and slain." The world stands guilty before God of the murder of His Son, and if you have never yet turned to God in repentance, saying, "O God, I confess the awful sin of rejecting Thy Son, and I take Him now as my Savior and own Him as my Lord," you remain under the dreadful indictment of having crucified the Lord of glory, for you stand with those who were guilty of the most fearful crime that has ever taken place in this world. Every man or woman who has never turned from the world to Christ stands guilty before God of the murder of His Son.

Do you say, "Preacher, you do not know me; I am respectable; my life is a good life; I am a good father, a good husband, a dutiful son, an obedient daughter. You have no reason to point me out as a sinner?" The Spirit came that He might convict men of sin. What sin? Jesus says, "Of sin, because they believe not on me" (John 16:9). If you are not guilty of any other sin, that one sin of Christ-rejection is the worst one you could possibly commit. And it is the sin that will sink you down to the deepest depths of bitter woe for all eternity if you do not repent, if you do not turn to God and say, "O God, I accept the One the world rejected, the One the world crucified. I put my trust in Him; I will take Him as my Savior." This is what Peter drove home in the power of the Holy Ghost to those people that day. He reminded them of what David said, "I have set the Lord always before me; because he is at my right hand, I shall not be moved," and then went on to show how this was fulfilled in Christ. "For thou wilt not leave my soul in hell, neither wilt thou suffer thine Holy One to see corruption." David was not speaking of himself, for he died and had to await the time when believers would be raised in the first resurrection. But Peter said that David was speaking of Christ, and he declared, "Therefore being a prophet, and knowing that God had sworn with an oath to him, that of the fruit of his loins, according to the flesh, he would raise up Christ to sit on his throne; He seeing this before spake of the resurrection of Christ, that his soul was not left in hell, neither his flesh did see corruption." Then Peter said, "This Jesus hath God raised up, whereof we all are witnesses."

Jesus has been raised from the dead. What does that mean? Two things. First, that He who died lives again to be Judge of all. "He hath appointed a day in which he will judge the world in righteousness by that man whom he hath ordained; whereof he hath given assurance unto all men, in that he hath raised him from the dead" (Acts 17:31). You must see Him some day; you must look into His face some day; must hear His voice, and meet Him either in this world or in the world to come.

The second thing is this: Jesus has been raised from the dead to give repentance and remission of sins. "Let all the house of Israel—(let all the people of Chicago)—know assuredly, that God hath made that same Jesus . . . both Lord and Christ." As Christ, He is the Savior of sinners, the risen Jesus. You must meet Him either in life or at the great white throne, but the first time you meet Him you must meet Him in all your sins. You can meet Him in your sins today and be saved for all eternity; but if you refuse to meet Him in your sins in this life, you must do so in the judgment day, only to hear Him say so sadly, so sorrowfully, "Depart from me; I never knew you."

Jesus lives. He lives to save you today if you will come to Him. This was the message that Peter preached. Can you imagine the results? Does it seem impossible that three thousand people smitten to the heart cried out, "What shall we do?" They confessed Jesus as Savior and Lord and were baptized in His name, and the same glorious gift was given to them as came to the twelve and to the one hundred and twenty. You have heard the same story. What effect will it have upon you? Are you here in your sin? Are you here unsaved? You cannot do a thing to save yourself, but Christ died for your sin and has been raised from the dead. He sits today exalted on God's right hand, a Prince and a Savior, and He has commissioned us to preach repentance and remission of sins to all who trust His name. Will you trust Him as did they of Pentecost over nineteen hundred years ago? Will you heed the message? Will you come to Him?

CHAPTER SIX

Consistent Christian Behavior

When thou buildest a new house, then thou shalt make a battlement for thy roof, that thou bring not blood upon thine house, if any man fall from thence. Thou shalt not sow thy vineyard with divers seeds; lest the fruit of thy seed which thou hast sown, and the fruit of thy vineyard, be defiled. Thou shalt not plow with an ox and an ass together. Thou shalt not wear a garment of divers sorts, as of woolen and linen together. Thou shalt make thee fringes upon the four quarters of thy vesture, wherewith thou coverest thyself.

(DEUTERONOMY 22:8-12)

As an amplification of the last verse in the above passage, let us turn to Numbers 15:37-38, where we read: "And the Lord spake unto Moses, saying, Speak unto the children of Israel, and bid them that they make them fringes in the borders of their garments throughout their generations, and that they put upon the fringe of the borders a ribband of blue." The apostle Paul set us the example of drawing spiritual lessons from some of these Old Testament regulations for which, otherwise, we might not see the need in our day. When he wrote of the support of Christian ministers, he went back to Deuteronomy to find a text. He selected one that we might think had no real application to the subject in hand—a very peculiar text indeed, "Thou shalt not muzzle the ox that treadeth out the corn" (Deuteronomy 25:4). We might naturally ask, What has that to do with the question of the support of a minister of the gospel? But Paul used it, not to teach consideration for the toiling creatures who so patiently serve man, though this is clearly emphasized in Scripture, but rather to show us our responsibility to care for the temporal needs of spiritual laborers, in order that they may be free to carry on their work without anxiety as to earthly things.

We read in Proverbs 12:10, "A righteous man regardeth the life of his beast: but the tender mercies of the wicked are cruel." A man who had been converted gave his testimony to that fact at a public meeting. When he finished, his wife stepped up and said, "My friends, if any one here questions my husband's testimony, you should come out to our farm. Before he was converted, every cow, every horse, and every dog on the place would run away from him because he was so vicious and would beat them so cruelly; now, all the animals run to him." The man's whole attitude toward the creatures of the farm was changed. But the apostle Paul says that this was not written just for the oxen, but for our benefit. The oxen treading out the corn is a beautiful picture of the servant of Christ—beating out the soul-nourishing truth of the Word of God in order that he may pass it on to us. Now think of the ox treading out the corn, and reaching down every now and then to pick up a bite for himself. God says, that they who preach the gospel should live of the gospel. Too many churches forget that. They are quite content to have the servants of Christ minister the Word year in and year out, and are not concerned in the least as to how they are cared for. They are like the deacon who prayed, "Lord, bless our minister; keep him humble, and we will keep him poor." The apostle's use of that text suggests many texts applying to by-gone conditions, which, after all, have a hidden suggestion for us.

These five verses of our text in Deuteronomy prove this in a remarkable way. "When thou buildest a new house, then thou shalt make a battlement for thy roof, that thou bring not blood upon thine house, if any man fall from thence." The roofs of the Hebrews' houses, as the roofs of many Oriental houses today, or the roofs of the Pueblo Indians and the Mexicans of our own country, served as places of social intercourse, where the families gathered to visit. The roof answered the same purpose that our living room does. In fact, the Hebrew could have well called the roof his parlor, a place of communion and fellowship. Samuel took Saul up on the roof and talked to him; he put food before him and bade him eat. The roof also was a place of prayer, for we read that the apostle Peter was praying on the roof of the house when he received the vision of the sheet that was suspended from heaven—a picture of the mystery of the church. Sometimes we go too far in saying that the mystery of the church was revealed only to the apostle Paul. The "all manner of beasts" represented the Gentiles' right to the gospel, afterward made expressly clear to Paul. God said, "When you build a new house you are to put a battlement around your roof." What for? Lest anybody should fall from thence. But here is a Hebrew who says, "I don't think a battlement will fit in with my plan of architecture. Besides, my wife and I are both elderly people. There is no danger for either of us. I will make a roof with a plain edge without any battlement." Before long some neighbor comes to visit them. They have a child of tender years, who, in running and playing about on the roof, comes too near the edge and goes over. Why did God order a battlement about the roof? Simply for this reason: the battlement afforded protection for all. This man is held responsible for the death of the child. The battlement may not always be for your own sake, but for the sake of other people. Does it not emphasize the New Testament words, "For none of us liveth to himself, and no man dieth to himself"? A great many things that we, as individuals, think we could do with impunity would wreck the Christian life of somebody weaker in faith. The fact that he sees us do something which he fears is not right or consistent with a Christian profession may lead him to do the same thing, but his consecration does not stand the strain—worldly things soon overcome him and his testimony as a Christian is lost. You can see, therefore, that your example was not right. An evil example has doubtless been the cause of much backsliding. In 1 Corinthians 8 we read of meat being offered to idols. Paul said that the Christian should not eat such meat if it would offend a weak one; we should do nothing to offend one of these. But, you say, "I can take that nice, tender steak. I can eat it and enjoy it even though it has been dedicated to the idol, for I know an idol is nothing but a mere lifeless image." "Yes, I know," says Paul, "but somebody else might drift away from Christianity if he saw you do it. Ruin not him for whom Christ died." We should live for others; we should be willing to sacrifice much in order to help others, and not mislead them.

"Thou shalt not sow thy vineyard with divers seeds; lest the fruit of thy seed which thou hast sown, and the fruit of thy vineyard, be defiled." Seed? For us, that means the Word of God. We have been entrusted with the Word of God, holy and free from error. Do not use "divers seeds." I want to warn you against dabbling with false cults. Some think they must be up-to-date, so they read everything and study everything that they can get their hands on in order that they may be well read. Often doubts are instilled in the mind in regard to great truths of God's Word, all because the vineyard has been sown with mingled seed. In 2 Kings 4:38-41 we read of Elisha preparing a meal for the sons of the prophets. Finances were not too abundant, so he sent them out into the field to gather some greens for dinner; by mistake, they gathered some that were poisonous. One of the students was a good taster, and it happened that, before they ate, he reached down and tasted death in the pot. Elisha was informed of the fact, and the greens were omitted from the menu. One spoonful proved that death was there. Some people think you have to go to the bottom of the pot in order to really test out what is in it. Someone says, "I believe in investigating; I can get a little good out of everything. I look into all religions and I find a little good in all of them. I listen to this one and that one and I can get a little good from all." Suppose we admit that. Our digestive organs might be able to assimilate stewed or boiled sawdust and possibly get a little nourishment from it, if there is any. But what a fool I would be to eat sawdust, when I could get good oatmeal porridge! Why not give yourself that which you know is nourishing? "Thou shalt not sow thy vineyard with mingled seed lest it be defiled." That is why the apostle wrote: "Study to show thyself approved unto God, a workman that needeth not to be ashamed, rightly dividing the word of truth" (2 Timothy 2:15).

Have you ever noticed in some preaching an absolute lack of definiteness? I was in a school recently where a man talked very indefinitely. At the close of his message, a youth asked me this question, "Is he a modernist or a fundamentalist?" I had to answer, "I do not know." There was nothing absolutely wrong, yet he did not say anything that any modernist could not have approved; it would not have killed a fly; it didn't amount to anything. Preach the truth in its simplicity. Don't get off on other lines.

The next verse is a warning against the unequal yoke. "Thou shalt not plow with an ox and an ass together." When the apostle wrote in 2 Corinthians 6:14, "Be not unequally yoked together with unbelievers," he must have had this passage in mind. An ox and a donkey, unsuited to each other, together—a stalwart old ox and a donkey are an unequal arrangement. Why? The ox is a clean beast, used for sacrifice, and the ass is an unclean beast, a type of the natural man. That is the trouble with all of us; by nature, we are just stubborn donkeys. The donkey nature will come out in us sometimes, even after conversion. We may say that the ass is a type of the sinner, the man in his natural condition; the ox is a picture of the servant of God. "Thou shalt not plow with an ox and an ass together." How far does this go? It touches every relationship in life. A Christian man has an opportunity to buy his way into a well-paying business. It means partnership with an ungodly man. How long does he do business without feeling the yoke vexing him? They are not fitted to work together. Such an arrangement generally culminates in the backsliding of the Christian—unless he breaks away. Some think that this does not apply to fraternal relationships. Often when I finish preaching, men will come to me and shake my hand in all kinds of strange ways. Do you belong to a fraternal organization? I belong to the greatest one on earth! The church of the living God is a wonderful society—a secret society of the mysteries that the world knows nothing about. Why have I not joined human fraternal organizations? Several Scriptures have kept me out. I am to take the Lord Jesus as my example. He said, "In secret I have said nothing." I have to follow Him. Then there is this question of the unequal yoke. And God has said, "Have no fellowship with the unfruitful works of darkness" (Ephesians 5:11). We belong to the light. What place have we in the secret lodge room?

Then there is the question of church fellowship. The bane of the professing church is its effort to get numbers. Get the people into the church and afterwards get them converted—build up a church membership. Where, in God's Word, do you read of the apostles of our Lord trying to get the unsaved into church fellowship? Where in the Word do you read that you must get the unregenerate in the church first, and then do them good afterwards? Ordinarily it works out as in the case of the boys who caught young linnets and placed one on one side and one on the other side of the canary. They told their mother that they had caught them young and placed them there by the canary so that they would learn to sing as did the canary. The mother was rather dubious, but she did not say anything. A few days later the boys rushed to their mother and cried, "Mother, our canary is chirping like a linnet." The linnets never learned to sing as the canary, but the canary lost its song. Christians become exceedingly worldly by association in church fellowship with the worldly. Be sure people are saved, and then lead them on into Christian fellowship.

This applies also to the marriage relationship. I never can understand how a real Christian can contemplate entering into the most sacred of all relationships with an unsaved person. Some seem to imagine that once married, they will be able to lead their partners to Christ. It generally goes the other way. After the honeymoon the unsaved one says, "I am not going to church any more, or have any more of that religious cant in my home." The unsaved one is usually the stronger. The other one has already disobeyed Christ, so he has not much spiritual strength by which to stand. An old Puritan divine once said, "If you marry a child of the devil, you can expect to have trouble with your father-in-law." "Thou shalt not plow with an ox and an ass together."

Deuteronomy 22:11 should come home to us, for it is about clothes. "Thou shalt not wear a garment of divers sort, as of woolen and linen together." Isn't it strange that God would not allow His people to wear mixed clothes? It was all right to wear linen and woolen if they were different garments, but not one in which the two were mixed. I want to call your attention to the word *garment* in this verse. In the Bible the word is used in two ways, meaning both clothing and behavior. Also in our English language, as well as in the Bible, *garment* and *behavior* are the same word; we have "habit" in clothing and "habit" in behavior. There are walking habits, riding habits, and bathing habits. We say, "That young man has a very evil habit," or "a good habit," meaning, of course, good behavior. Clothing then represents behavior. We speak of someone's garments always being white. What is that? Behavior. "Fine linen" is the righteousnesses of the saints. The Bride has made herself ready by righteous behavior. The sinner's righteousnesses are as filthy rags, just like old, defiled garments. Now God says to you and to me: "You are not to be people of mixed behavior, very pious and godly in the classroom and thoroughly worldly and carnal outside; religious in church and very frivolous and foolish in the world—not to have one behavior in one company and another in another company." Remember, wherever you find yourself, that you are there to represent the Lord Jesus Christ. Take Lot for an example. Lot wore garments of linen and woolen. When with Abraham, he was very saintly, but in Sodom there was not much difference between him and the crowd. He was thought so well of, in fact, that they elected him a judge. They never would have made Abraham a judge.

Let us think for a moment, on worldly pleasures. No Christian who is walking with God is troubled much concerning them. In the first place, the world doesn't want them around. Gypsy Smith, the great evangelist, in a sermon one night, danced across the stage, and then said, "My friends, I can dance as well as any of you, but since the day I was converted, nobody has invited me to a dance or to the theater." Why hadn't they? Because they knew from the day of his conversion that he was out and out for God! Your conversion has killed your chances with the world. Can't you hear some worldly friend saying, "There isn't any use asking her. She will throw gloom all over the party, talking about our souls. Imagine her getting you into some corner and saying, 'Is your soul saved?'" If you wear the right kind of garments, you will never be in style with the world.

Now we will look at the positive side of this question. "Thou shalt make thee fringes upon the four quarters of thy vesture, wherewith thou coverest thyself." "And the Lord spake unto Moses, saying, Speak unto the children of Israel, and bid them that they make them fringes in the borders of their garments throughout their generations, and that they put upon the fringes of the borders a ribband of blue" (Numbers 15:37-38). The Lord Jesus undoubtedly dressed that way. But why the ribbon of blue? In order "that ye may remember, and do all my commandments, and be holy unto your God." God says to His people, "You are to be characterized by heavenly-mindedness in all your ways." Are you always careful to have the ribbon of blue? Do people realize that you belong to Heaven? Our citizenship, you know, is in Heaven. "If ye then be risen with Christ, seek those things which are above, where Christ sitteth on the right hand of God. Set your affection on things above, not on things on the earth" (Colossians 3:1-2). The Israelite had this band of blue around the lower edge of his garment (he always wore long flowing garments), so that right down to the very lowest place where the garment nearly touched the earth he wore that which showed he belonged to the God of Heaven. Where you and I come closest to the world, we are to manifest the heavenly character. Can you say, "For to me to live is Christ"? Who lives Christ? One who wears a ribbon of blue!

It has been told how, years ago, the Crown Prince of France was put under the care of an English tutor. The Dauphin was of royal blood and his tutor was of ordinary strain. It was unthinkable that a commoner should attempt to punish one of royal blood, and yet the prince was often as obnoxious as he could be; he made life as difficult for the English tutor as possible. In despair at last, hardly knowing how to control his royal pupil, the Englishman had a purple rosette made, and the next morning at the appearance of the prince, he said, "I want to pin this on your coat." "What's that for?" "That is the royal color. It is not permitted me to punish you for any disobedience of the rules, but whenever you misbehave, I am going to point at the purple." Then one day the prince acted in an ungentlemanly way; he was naughty. The tutor stopped, pointed to the purple, and immediately the prince colored and said, "I beg your pardon." It was the appeal to the purple, reminding the Dauphin that rank imposes obligation. God gives us an appeal—it is an appeal to the blue. We represent Heaven. The world judges our Lord by us.

> You are writing a Gospel, a chapter each day,
> By deeds that you do, by words that you say;
> Men read what you write, whether faithful or true—
> Say, what is the Gospel, according to you?

Chapter Seven

The Priesthood of All Believers

By him therefore let us offer the sacrifice of praise to God continually, that is, the fruit of our lips giving thanks to his name. But to do good and to communicate forget not: for with such sacrifices God is well pleased.
(HEBREWS 13:15-16)

The thought of a distinct priesthood of a certain class separated from their brethren and occupying a peculiar place of nearness to God is utterly foreign to the New Testament. All believers are designated priests in this dispensation. In Revelation 1:6 the apostle said that He "hath made us kings and priests unto God and his Father," and the *us* there clearly takes in all the redeemed family in this wonderful dispensation of grace. The apostle Peter, too, wrote that we are "holy priests" and "royal priests"; and he was not speaking of any special grace resting upon the apostolic company or upon any peculiar class set apart to some sacerdotal office, but he spoke of all believers. He said that we are holy and royal priests, and Paul, who I believe was the writer of the Epistle to the Hebrews, told us that we are to offer up "spiritual sacrifices."

Sacrificing is a priestly function. In Old Testament times the people of God were divided into three classes; there were some priests, others ministers or Levites, and the rest were warriors. There were those especially set apart as worshipers and others as ministers on behalf of God to His people. The priest, you see, goes in to God on behalf of the people; the Levite goes out to the people on behalf of God. Then there were those who were called upon to contend for the rights of the people of God and for the glory of God—they were warriors. However, in the New Testament dispensation every believer is a warrior; we are called upon to "contend earnestly for the faith which was once delivered unto the saints" (Jude 3). Every believer is also a minister; we all have some gift, and "as every man hath received the gift, even so minister the same one to another, as good stewards of the manifold grace of God" (I Peter 4:10). We are called upon to labor for the blessing of a lost world. Then, thirdly, we are all priests; we are all worshipers, and it is the privilege of each one of us to enter where the ordinary priests of old never could enter, into the holiest, where we come in all the infinite value of the precious atoning blood of our Lord Jesus Christ.

Now worship is the very highest exercise of the human spirit, but it is that of which we know the least, and to which most of us give the least attention. We all know what it means to fight for the truth, to contend for the Word. I take it that most of us realize the tremendous responsibility resting upon us in these days of declension and apostasy to stand firmly for the truth of God, to be ready to defend that truth even if it should mean to lay down our lives for it. We know something of real ministry, to serve our brethren or to serve by carrying the gospel to the world. But some of us, I fear, imagine that when we have stood valiantly for the truth and ministered to the needs of others, that is about all that God is looking for from us. He said to the woman at the well, "God is a Spirit: and they that worship him must worship him in spirit and in truth" (John 4:24), "for the Father seeketh such to worship him" (John 4: 23). Have you ever thought very much about that?

You recall that wonderful word in Luke 19:10: "The Son of man is come to seek and to save that which was lost." Our blessed Lord, a Seeker! And whom is He seeking? He is seeking after lost men and women to bring them to the knowledge of redemption. And where does He seek? Out in the world, everywhere wherever man is found. But now we see that God the Father is a Seeker. For whom is He seeking? The Father seeketh worshipers. And where does He go to seek worshipers? Out in the wide world? Oh, no! Men talk, you know, about public worship. The public cannot worship; the greater part of the public are lost sinners trampling on the Savior's blood and going on to endless judgment. They are not worshipers. It is not out in the world where the Father is looking for worshipers; but where does He look? Among the redeemed! When people have been washed from their sins in the precious blood of Christ; when they have been cleansed from sin's pollution, then—think of it!—among them the Father is seeking worshipers! After all, there are so few even of the bloodwashed who rise to the heights of their privileges and responsibilities and take their rightful place as priests before God.

You know the priest is the worshiper. Men are often content when they come into what is called a religious service to let the man in the pulpit do the praying and the preaching, and the choir do the singing, and they just sit and look on and then go away and say, "We have been worshiping God," and perhaps all the time God was seeking through that audience for worshipers and hardly finding any.

You remember the ten lepers that came to Christ in their need, pleading that they might be healed. He said, "Go show yourselves unto the priests." What was the meaning of that? In Leviticus 13 and 14, where we have the regulations in regard to leprosy, we are told that when a leper was cleansed, he was to go and show himself to the priest and offer sacrifice. But do you realize that in all the fifteen hundred years that had rolled by since God had inspired Moses to write those chapters, there is no record that they had ever been acted upon? No man at any time ever came to a priest in Israel and said, "See, I was a leper, but I have been healed and I have brought my sacrifice." So that part of the law of God had become a dead letter to the priests in Israel; but how astonished they must have been when the people began coming, first one and then another, and said, "I want you to examine me; I have been a leper for years, but I have been healed, and I have come to bring the sacrifice." I imagine some of the priests must have been greatly perturbed! I fancy some of them were so astonished that they did not know what to do. They probably went back to consult the Book, as they said, "Why, we have never heard of this before; of course it is in the Bible but we have had no occasion to look into this particular instruction. Who healed you?" they would ask. And to their amazement and perhaps chagrin, the answer would come, "Jesus, the Prophet of Nazareth; He touched me and made me whole, and I have come to bring the offering according to the law."

What a wonderful thing that was—those ten lepers pleaded that they might be healed, and Jesus said, "Go show yourselves unto the priests." What did that mean? Here they were covered with leprosy. "Well," one might say, "He told us to go, and He must mean that by the time we get there everything will be all right," and so they had faith enough to go, and they were healed.

But one of the lepers suddenly felt a strange sensation come over him and he looked at his hands and said, "My word! I have not seen my hands look like that for years, these hands that were so covered with leprosy. Did you notice anything different about me?" "Why," they might have said, "you were never so good-looking in your life. We are healed; we are well; the leprosy is gone!" And nine of them went off to the temple in accordance with the Word, but one of them, a Samaritan, said, "Why should I go to that temple? There is One here greater than the temple. I am going back to Him," and back he went and fell down at the feet of the blessed Lord, a worshiper—a worshiper! Do you get that? He fell down to adore, to bless, to thank the One who had healed him, and how the heart of Jesus was touched as He exclaimed, "Were there not ten cleansed? but where are the nine? There are not found that returned to give glory to God, save this stranger" (Luke 17:17-18).

This is the picture of a worshiper, and that is what the priest is, and when the Word of God tells us that we are all priests, it means that we are all set apart as worshipers. After Aaron and his sons were first thus consecrated every son in their families was born a priest. And dear friends, there is no human ordinance or ceremonial service that will make a priest of you today; you must be born a priest. "But," you say, "it is all up with me then; for I was born into an ungodly family." Oh, but that is where the Word of the Lord comes in. "Ye must be born again," and when you are born the second time, you are born into the priestly family. Aaron was at the head of his family and all his sons were called "his house." Now Christ is the head of the priestly family today, and all who receive life through Christ are called "His house."

But before the priest could enter upon his service there were certain ceremonies through which he had to go. First, he was brought to the door of the tabernacle; and that is typical. Jesus says, "I am the door; by me if any man enter in, he shall be saved" (John 10:9). The priest is a man who has a personal acquaintance with Christ. Dear friend, do you know Him, that blessed One who is the way into the very presence of God and who says, "No man cometh unto the Father but by me"? Come to the Door!

Next, he was stripped of all his secular garments; and for every one of us there has to be the stripping. Saul of Tarsus, in his unconverted days, thought he was well dressed. In Philippians 3, he told us of the many things in which he used to glory, and then he had a vision of the Savior, and stripping took place. "What things were gain to me," he said, "those I counted loss for Christ" (Philippians 3:7). Some of us remember when we labored pretty hard to get "well dressed" in order to fit ourselves for God. We did not like denying ourselves all these things, but when Christ filled the vision of our soul, then we could say, "God forbid that I should glory, save in the cross of our Lord Jesus Christ" (Galatians 6:14). Paul said that I may "be found in him, not having mine own righteousness, which is of the law, but that which is through the faith of Christ, the righteousness which is of God by faith" (Philippians 3:9).

I was talking to a large group at a college one day, and an illustration came to my mind which will probably not fit you all quite so well. I said, "Just imagine one of you girls working your way through college. You have very little spending money; your parents are not able to provide for you; possibly you have no parents. There is going to be some great affair and all are supposed to be nicely dressed for this occasion, and you do not like to be shabby, but you have so little to go on. Then you see that at the five and ten cent store, there is a splendid sale on material for ten cents a yard. You have only a few dimes, but you go down and get a few yards and try to make a nice little gown so that you can go to that function. But you have never had much training as a seamstress and you have a lot of trouble. However, you work away on it trying to make it look respectable. Then one day Lady Bountiful visits you; you have always dreamed about her but never expected to see her. She takes a kindly interest in you and says, "Look, I want you to go downtown with me." You go, wondering why she should be interested in you, and then she takes you into one of the most beautiful establishments of the city. You are stirred as you walk up and down those aisles, and as she stops at the dress section, she says, "Now, my dear, pick out any dress you please; a gown for yourself, any one that you like." "Well, really," you say, "that seems too good to be true. I am afraid my taste would lead me to pick out something too expensive." But she says, "Go right on—anything you want." And so your fancy for color leads you to select a certain one and you say, "Well, I think that would be very becoming." "All right," she says, and to the saleslady, "How much is it?" The answer is, "Seventy-five dollars." "Oh," you say, "that is altogether beyond a poor girl like me." "But that is all right, you like it and you are going to have it." Imagine the girl coming back to her little room seeing the poor old figured goods at which she had been working so long. She gets the new one out and tries it on and parades up and down before the glass. Finally she calls in the other girls and says, "Oh, now I shall be found not having my own dress, this poor inexpensive thing, but this beautiful gown, that has been given to me so freely!" Do you see it?

Paul looked at it that way. He had been trying to work out his righteousness himself, trying to make a beautiful garment in which to stand before God; but when he got sight of the risen Christ, and learned that every believer is made the righteousness of God in Christ, he said, "Away with that thing of my own providing, now that I can be dressed up in the righteousness which is of God in Christ."

Yes, we have to be stripped, but before we put on the new clothes there is something more. We find the priests were bathed all over. That speaks of cleansing, every whit. When I come to the place where I am willing to let go my own righteousness and put my trust in Christ, I am washed from every sin stain and made clean. "Now ye are clean through the word which I have spoken unto you" (John 15:3). The Word tells me of atoning blood shed for my sins on Calvary's tree—"And the blood of Jesus Christ his Son cleanseth us from all sin" (1 John 1:7). I am not only made clean but I am clothed; now it is that God puts upon me this robe, a divine righteousness, and I can exclaim with Isaiah, "He hath clothed me with the garments of salvation, He hath covered me with the robe of righteousness" (Isaiah. 61:10).

Now I am ready to enter upon my office as a priest. What do I do? The priest was a worshiper. Of old he offered sacrifice for sin, but we have no sacrifice for sin to offer because our great High Priest settled that when He offered up Himself. But what do I offer now? The priest offered the gifts of a grateful people as well. The people came bringing their gifts, and he presented them before the Lord, and so you and I come bringing our gifts. "By him therefore let us offer the sacrifice of praise to God continually, that is, the fruit of our lips giving thanks to his name" (Hebrews 13:15).

Did you ever notice that rather odd expression in Hosea 14:2, "So will we render the calves of our lips"? The people of old presented their cattle to God, but the prophet looking on into the future saw that we will have no calf to burn, but exclaimed, "We will render the calves of our lips." We are coming to God pleading the infinite value of the Lord Jesus and praising Him for the grace that led Him to stoop so low as to save us. We bring Christ to God as the praise of our hearts.

In Deuteronomy 26 there is a lovely picture. When the people of Israel came into the land, they were to take a basket of the firstfruits and set it down before the Lord; and the priest (you see they could not go any further) was to bring it in and set it in the presence of the Lord, and the people were to confess that they themselves were poor sinners but God had dealt with them in lovingkindness. And so we come today bringing our baskets of firstfruits.

And Christ Himself is the "firstfruits," we are told. He is the sample sheaf of the coming great harvest. We shall all be like Him some day. Meantime we come to God bringing to Him the One in whom He delights and we now delight in Him too.

But now it is not just this one side. Peter said that we are holy priests and royal priests. "Ye also, as [living] stones, are built up a spiritual house, an holy priesthood, to offer up spiritual sacrifices acceptable to God by Jesus Christ" (1 Peter 2:5), that is, to offer the praises of thanksgiving, of adoration to God "acceptable by Christ Jesus." And that is not all.

He not only said we are holy priests (not in any holiness of our own), but in 1 Peter 2:9 he said, "Ye are a chosen generation, a royal priesthood, an holy nation, a peculiar people; that ye should shew forth the praises of him who hath called you out of darkness into his marvelous light." As a holy priest I go in to God to worship; as a royal priest (linked up with my Melchizedek priest-king), I go out before men to show forth the praises of Him who has called me "out of darkness into his marvelous light." And how do I do that? By manifesting Christ to men. I bring Christ to God and come into His presence as a worshiper with a heart enraptured with Christ, and then I take Christ out to men and show to others what God has given me.

First, "By him therefore let us offer the sacrifice of praise to God continually, that is, the fruit of our lips giving thanks to his name" (Hebrews 13:15). Now look at the other side, "But to do good and to communicate (to share what you have with others whether in things spiritual or temporal) forget not; for with such sacrifices God is well pleased" (Hebrews 13:16).

Thus we have the two sides to our worship. We honor God by offering the sacrifice of praise through Christ, and we prove that we are true worshipers by manifesting the love of God to those in need.

Chapter Eight

The Presentation of First Fruits

A Thanksgiving Day Sermon

By him therefore let us offer the sacrifice of praise to God continually, that is, the fruit of our lips giving thanks to his name. But to do good and to communicate forget not; for with such sacrifices God is well pleased.
(HEBREWS *13:15-16*)

(Deuteronomy 26 was read as a Scripture lesson. If our readers will open their Bibles to that chapter and keep it before them, they will follow the sermon with greater clearness.)

In Deuteronomy 26 we have what undoubtedly gave rise to the Puritans' harvest home festival. It was Israel's national Thanksgiving Day and most suggestive of that which should occupy our hearts at this present time. You will notice the chapter is divided into two parts. In verses 1 to 11, the people are seen bringing the first fruits to God and rejoicing before Him as they give thanks for all the mercies of the past year. In verses 12 to 19, the same people are seen ministering to the Levites, the strangers, the fatherless, and the widows, and to all who are poor and needy among them, and by these acts of consideration for their less fortunate fellowmen and for the servants of the Lord, who were largely dependent upon their bounty, we see evidences of grace working in their souls, and can understand something of what our own attitude ought to be when, blessed ourselves, we look upon a vast host who are suffering for the lack of what God has so graciously lavished upon us.

These two divisions of this great chapter answer to the two aspects of sacrifice brought before us in our text. In Hebrews 13:15 we have the sacrifice of praise to God; the fruit of lips that confess the name of Jesus. Whereas in verse 16 we have the sacrifice of ministering to those in need; doing good and sharing with others what God has given to us.

This sacrifice of praise can be presented to God only by those who are in happy relationship with Himself. None but redeemed people can come into His holy presence as worshipers. Worship is not merely the observance of some religious ceremony; neither does it consist in listening to a sermon, nor in presenting our petitions in prayer. It is a great mistake to think of worship as the enjoyment of soulful and beautiful music. Carnal and even unconverted people may have their sentimental natures thoroughly aroused by the dulcet strains of the organ or by the sweet singing of a trained choir. But this enjoyment does not necessarily imply that the spirit is worshiping God in reality. Our Lord Himself said to the Samaritan woman, "God is a Spirit, and they that worship him must worship him in spirit and in truth." The highest worship is when the saint of God enters by faith into the holiest, passing through the rent veil and prostrating himself before the throne of the Eternal, there to gaze with adoring love and gratitude upon our blessed Lord Jesus Christ who now sits exalted on the Father's throne. There can be no true worship apart from our occupation with Himself. Outward observances may often hinder rather than help because there is ever the danger of distracting the mind, of fixing the attention upon some religious performance instead of on Christ Himself. It is when the spirit enters into the stillness, the quiet of God's own presence, there to be overwhelmed with a sense of the divine holiness and the divine love as manifested in the Lord Jesus Christ, that we really worship.

And this is pictured for us very beautifully in Deuteronomy 26:1-11. We read in verses 1 and 2: "And it shall be, when thou art come in unto the land which the Lord thy God giveth thee for an inheritance, and possessest it, and dwellest therein: That thou shalt take of the first of all the fruit of the earth, which thou shalt bring of thy land that the Lord thy God giveth thee, and shalt put it in a basket, and shalt go unto the place which the Lord thy God shall choose to place his name there." Observe this was something that could never be carried out in the wilderness, and certainly not in Egypt. God says, "When thou art come in unto the land." As a redeemed people, redeemed by blood and redeemed by power, dwelling in the inheritance which God had given them, the Israelites were called to observe this festival. No unsaved person, no one who is still in nature's darkness and in bondage to sin and Satan, no one who has not been washed from his sins in the blood of Jesus and raised up together and made to sit together in heavenly places in Christ can be a true worshiper. Men often speak of public worship, but this is a mistake. The public cannot worship. Worship is a very selective thing, and it is the glad privilege of those who are complete in Christ.

Now notice the form their service was to take. They were commanded to bring the first fruits of the land which the Lord had given them; to put it in a basket; and to go to the place where the Lord had chosen to set His name. How significant all this is. The first fruits speak of Christ Himself, even as we read in 1 Corinthians 15:20: "But now is Christ risen from the dead and become the first fruits of them that slept." Again in verse 23: "Christ the first fruits; afterwards they that are Christ's at his coming." The first fruits tell of the great harvest soon to be gathered in, even as a risen Christ has entered into the presence of God as our forerunner, the pledge of the great ingathering when millions of the redeemed will be transformed and translated at the moment of His return.

The basket may well speak of our poor hearts, limited indeed as we often are in ourselves, and yet in which Christ is pleased to dwell, "that Christ may dwell in your hearts by faith." We come to God with a heart filled with Christ, thinking of Him, praising Him, occupied alone with Him, rejoicing in Jesus Christ and having no confidence in the flesh. How God delights to see His people thus before Him.

I was trying to expound this passage some years ago and there was a dear little golden-haired girl present. On the way home she said to her father, "Daddy, I didn't have anything in my basket for the Lord today." Thinking she had not understood, the father said, "Well, Flossy, what do you mean?" "I was so busy," she said, "going to school and playing, that I didn't put anything in my basket." "You didn't?" the father asked, still not sure that she had understood. "No," she said, and walked along silently for a few moments, and then said, "Daddy, I am going to have my basket full by next Sunday." "How are you going to get it full?" her father asked. "Every day," said the little one, "I am going to stop playing for a little while and think of Jesus, and I think by Sunday I will have it full." "Out of the mouth of babes and sucklings thou hast perfected praise" (Matthew 21:16). Yes, a heart filled with Christ, that constitutes a worshiper.

Of old there was only one place where the first fruits could be presented and that was at the place where God had set His name, where the tabernacle had been pitched, or later on, the temple built, and where He dwelt between the cherubim. Now it is to no earthly sanctuary we are invited to come, but the word is, "Having therefore, brethren, boldness to enter into the holiest by the blood of Jesus, By a new and living way, which he hath consecrated for us, through the veil, that is to say, his flesh: And having an high priest over the house of God: Let us draw near with a true heart in full assurance of faith, having our hearts sprinkled from an evil conscience, and our bodies washed with pure water" (Hebrews 10:19-22). Neither in Jerusalem, nor in some temple on a Samaritan mountain do we find God, but as a spiritual people, we enter in spirit into His immediate presence, and there present our first fruits.

Accompanied with the presentation, we have the confession as in verse 3: "And thou shalt go unto the priest that shall be in those days, and say unto him, I profess this day unto the Lord thy God, that I am come into the country which the Lord sware unto our fathers for to give us." It was a recognition and an acknowledgment of the fact that there had not failed one word of all God's good promise. And so today as a worshiping company, we gladly confess that we have by faith entered into the inheritance which is ours in Christ. The priest is another picture of our Lord Jesus Christ Himself. We read, "The priest shall take the basket out of thine hand, and set it down before the altar of the Lord thy God." It is our great High Priest who presents to God our worship and praises, and it is His perfection which alone can make our feeble adoration acceptable to the Father.

No thought of merit was to be in the mind of the Israelite and surely there can be none with us. We are saved by grace apart from works, and so have nothing of which to boast. Their confession was most abject: "A Syrian ready to perish was my father, and he went down into Egypt, and sojourned there with a few, and became there a nation, great, mighty, and populous: And the Egyptians evil entreated us, and afflicted us, and laid upon us hard bondage: And when we cried unto the Lord God of our fathers, the Lord heard our voice, and looked on our affliction and our labor, and our oppression: And the Lord brought us forth out of Egypt with a mighty hand, and with an outstretched arm, and with great terribleness, and with signs, and with wonders: And he hath brought us into this place, and hath given us this land, even a land that floweth with milk and honey. And now, behold, I have brought the firstfruits of the land, which thou, O Lord, hast given me. And thou shalt set it before the Lord thy God, and worship before the Lord thy God" (Deuteronomy 26:5-10).

What an acknowledgment was this that they owed every blessing to divine grace! They merited nothing, they purchased nothing, but all came to them through the wondrous lovingkindness of the Lord. And so in response to that matchless mercy, they brought the first fruits and set them down before Him, rejoicing in His presence because of all the good things He had lavished on them. Shall we not emulate them this morning as we think of a nobler inheritance, a greater deliverance, and a more marvelous exhibition of divine grace than they ever dreamed of, all ours in Christ Jesus? Surely we can rejoice in Him today and offer the fruit of lips that confess His name.

But what about the needy all around us? The spiritually needy and the temporally needy also? We have been blessed in Christ; and concerning earthly things, we are told, "He giveth us richly all things to enjoy." But at our very doors are those who know nothing of the grace of God revealed in Christ. All about us are those who are suffering for lack of the everyday mercies that mean so much to us. God has given us an example in His further commandment to Israel of what His pleasure is in regard to this. We read in Deuteronomy 26:12-14: "When thou hast made an end of tithing all the tithes of thine increase the third year, which is the year of tithing, and hast given it unto the Levite, the stranger, the fatherless, and the widow, that they may eat within thy gates, and be filled; Then thou shalt say before the Lord thy God, I have brought away the hallowed things out of mine house, and also have given them unto the

Levite, and unto the stranger, to the fatherless, and to the widow, according to all thy commandments which thou hast commanded me: I have not transgressed thy commandments, neither have I forgotten them: I have not eaten thereof in my mourning, neither have I taken away ought thereof for any unclean use, nor given ought thereof for the dead: but I have hearkened to the voice of the Lord my God, and have done according to all that thou hast commanded me." Here was grace in activity; here was love manifested. Here was the kindness of God seen in His people as they ministered to the need of others. In Hebrews 13:16 we have the same thing where God says, "But to do good and to communicate, forget not; for with such sacrifices God is well pleased." He would not have those who have been so richly blessed forget the needs of others, and I am quite sure that no one who truly enjoys Christ can help telling of Him to men and women who are still strangers to His grace. And as we thank God today for the temporal mercies He has lavished upon us, our enjoyment will be the greater as we share these good things with those whose circumstances are not so agreeable as ours, passing on to them what will brighten their lives and gladden their hearts in the name of Him who said, "It is more blessed to give than to receive."

You have heard of the old gentleman who was so pious that all through the church service he would sit with enraptured face looking up to heaven, but when they passed the collection plate he closed his eyes so as not to be disturbed in his meditation. Dear friends, spirituality is manifested just as truly in sharing with others what God has entrusted to us; whether it is making known the gospel or giving to others that which would alleviate their distress. But whoever sees his brother in need and says, "Depart in peace, be ye warmed and filled; notwithstanding ye give them not those things which are needful to the body; what doth it profit?" (James 2:16) You see, as priestly believers we are called upon to present our sacrifice of praise to God, and our sacrifice of giving to the world outside. May we truly enter into the responsibilities and the privileges of our priesthood, that the name of our Lord Jesus Christ may be magnified.

Chapter Nine

How Pontius Pilate Lost His Soul

Then said Pilate unto him, Speakest thou not unto me? knowest thou not that I have power to crucify thee and have power to release thee? Jesus answered, Thou couldest have no power at all against me, except it were given thee from above: therefore he that delivered me unto thee hath the greater sin. And from thenceforth Pilate sought to release him: but the Jews cried out, saying, If thou let this man go, thou art not Caesar's friend; whosoever maketh himself a king speaketh against Caesar. When Pilate therefore heard that saying, he brought Jesus forth, and sat down in the judgment seat in a place that is called the Pavement, but in the Hebrew, Gabbatha. And it was the preparation of the passover, and about the sixth hour: and he saith unto the Jews, Behold your King! But they cried out, Away with him, away with him, crucify him. Pilate saith unto them, Shall I crucify your King? The chief priests answered, We have no king but Caesar. Then delivered he him therefore unto them to be crucified. And they took Jesus and led him away.

(JOHN 19:10-16)

Four times in the New Testament outside of the Gospels, Pontius Pilate is mentioned by name. When Peter was preaching, after the healing of the lame man, as recorded in Acts 3:13: "The God of Abraham, and of Isaac, and of Jacob, the God of our fathers, hath glorified his Son Jesus; whom ye delivered up, and denied in the presence of Pilate, when he was determined to let him go." In Acts 4:27 we read, "For of a truth against thy holy child Jesus, whom thou hast anointed, both Herod and Pontius Pilate, with the Gentiles, and the people of Israel, were gathered together." In Acts 13:28 Paul, when preaching in the synagogue at Antioch, retold the story of the rejection of Christ, and he said, "And though they found no cause of death in him, yet desired they Pilate that he should be slain." Again in 1 Timothy 6:13-14 the apostle said to this young preacher, "I give thee charge in the sight of God, who quickeneth all things, and before Christ Jesus, who before Pontius Pilate witnessed a good confession; That thou keep this commandment without spot, unrebukable, until the appearing of our Lord Jesus Christ."

This man, Pontius Pilate, occupies a large place in the Word of God, and strikingly enough, there is perhaps no name better known next to the name of our Lord Jesus Christ than that of Pontius Pilate. Throughout all the Christian centuries, ever since the beginning of the second century when the so-called Apostles' Creed was compiled, thousands, and at times millions, of professed Christian people have recited Sunday after Sunday, "I believe in God the Father Almighty, Maker of heaven and earth and in Jesus Christ His Son who was conceived of the Holy Ghost, born of the virgin Mary, suffered under Pontius Pilate." And that man's name is going down to eternal infamy because of the stand he took when our Lord Jesus was brought before him for judgment.

Another name is intimately linked with that of Pilate in connection with the mock trial of our blessed Savior. It is that of Herod. He was a grossly carnal, depraved and immoral wretch whose vile life disgraced the title he bore. He lost his soul because of the sin of impurity, that same damning sin that is ruining so many today. It "has cast down many thousands; yea, many strong men have been slain by it." Everywhere it is prevalent, and until men judge the sin of impurity, until they come to the place where they are ready to be delivered from it, it is absolutely impossible to exercise saving faith in the Lord Jesus Christ. "Know ye not that the unrighteous shall not inherit the kingdom of God? Be not deceived: neither fornicators, nor idolaters, nor adulterers, nor effeminate, nor abusers of themselves with mankind, Nor thieves, nor covetous, nor drunkards, nor revilers, nor extortioners, shall inherit the kingdom of God" (1 Corinthians 6:9-10).

Men cannot be saved in their sins; they can be saved only when they are ready to judge their sins and to be delivered from them. Herod is the outstanding example of a man ruined for time and eternity through the sin of impurity. No such stain as that seems to be upon the life of Pontius Pilate. There is no intimation in Scripture nor yet in what has come down to us in secular history concerning this man, that he was an immoral or licentious man. But it is very evident that the sin that kept him from getting right with God was another one altogether, and yet one that is very common among us today. The sin that ruined Pilate was that of selfish ambition. This man was procurator of Judea and as such was vice-king and represented the authority of Rome in Judea from about A.D. 26 until A.D. 37. He was characterized by an overweening pride and ambition, and because of this he lost his soul.

If you are unsaved, what is the sin that is keeping you from Christ? Is it that you dread what men might think of you if you came to God as a poor sinner, put your trust in the Lord Jesus Christ, and confessed Him as your Savior? This was what destroyed Pilate. He went contrary to his conscience because he felt if he did not do so, he would lose his opportunities for advancement in the Roman Empire. The threat of the Jewish hierarchy, "If thou let this man go, thou art not Caesar's friend: whosoever maketh himself a king, speaketh against Caesar," was too much for Pilate.

It is very interesting to go back and read in the four Gospels the different accounts of what took place that morning when the Lord of life and glory stood before Pilate's judgment seat. During the previous night He had passed through His mock trial before Caiaphas and Caiaphas' father-in-law, Annas, and very early in the morning, about 7 o'clock our time, He was dragged into the presence of Pilate. The Roman governor had hardly finished his breakfast when the clamoring mob appeared in the door of the judgment hall. Not one of them was ready to put his foot across the threshold because it was the Passover time and they were so religious, so punctilious about ritual ceremonies, that they would not dare step into the house of a Gentile lest they should be defiled. Yet they were deliberately rejecting the Savior that God had provided for them. How many there are today who, just like these people, are very careful about religious observances, but still refuse to own themselves sinners and receive the Lord Jesus Christ as their Savior.

Pilate, hastily summoned, took his place upon the judgment seat. The Lord Jesus Christ was placed before him. Historians, theologians, and artists have tried to picture Him standing there. We read that the people led Him bound to Pilate, and generally the artists take it for granted that it was His wrists that were bound, but some tell us that the word in the original implies that it was a hangman's rope that was placed around His neck! They led Him ignominiously along with the murderer's halter around His neck! They dragged Him in that way into the presence of Pilate. Our friends of the Episcopal church and different branches of the Catholic church are accustomed to place around the neck of a clergyman what is called "the stole," and this has come down from ancient times as a reminder of the rope that was around the neck of the Son of God as He was dragged before Pilate. There He stood; He had made Himself a little lower than the angels with a view to the suffering of death; He had become a man, and now He takes the lowest place. He stands there condemned as a blasphemer by those He loved so tenderly, and they demand that Pilate pronounce the death sentence upon Him.

Conditions were such then that, in order to placate the Jews, it had been decreed that they might have the right of judgment in all cases having to do with the violation of their own laws; but the power of life and death rested with the Roman procurator. They had declared Jesus a blasphemer but had no authority to carry out their own judgment, and so came to Pilate that he might confirm it and put the Lord Jesus Christ to death. Pilate naturally asked the question, "What accusation bring ye against this man?" (John 18:29-30) They had no accusation which would stand in a Roman court; no accusation which would be of any value toward the condemnation of the prisoner. They answered, "If he were not a malefactor, we would not have delivered him up unto thee," as much as to say, "You insult us when you ask for an accusation. We would not have delivered Him unto you if we were not confident of His being a malefactor."

Pilate looked upon them with that contempt which the Romans always felt for the Hebrews, and said, "Very well, then, if you have no accusation, you take Him and judge Him according to your law." But they said, "It is not lawful for us to put any man to death." And Pilate looked on in wonder. He gazed on the face of the prisoner before him. What should he do with Him? He would have been as insensate as the marble images in his court, if his heart had not been moved by the plight of the prisoner, and so he entered the judgment hall again and called Jesus to him personally, and said, quietly, "Art thou the King of the Jews?" Jesus answered by putting a question to him, "Sayest thou this thing of thyself, or did others tell it thee of me?" In other words, "Are you asking Me this because of a real desire to know, or did somebody tell you that I am the King of the Jews?" Then Pilate said, "Am I a Jew?" And you can see the look of contempt on his face. "Thine own nation and the chief priests have delivered thee unto me: what hast thou done?" In other words, "They say you claim to be the King of the Jews; is this true?" Convinced that up to this point he is really an honest man in perplexity, Jesus makes that good confession of which John wrote, "My kingdom is not of this world [that is, not of this present order]: if my kingdom were of this world, then would my servants fight, that I should not be delivered to the Jews; but now is my kingdom not from hence" (John 18:36). Pilate looked up quickly and said, "Art thou a king then?" Jesus answered, "Thou sayest that I am a king. To this end was I born, and for this cause came I into the world, that I should bear witness unto the truth. Every one that is of the truth heareth my voice" (37). Here is a challenge.

When Jesus stood before Caiaphas He answered not a word until Caiaphas put Him on oath and said, "I adjure thee by the living God." Then Jesus replied, "Thou hast said; nevertheless I say unto you, Hereafter shall ye see the Son of man sitting on the right hand of power, and coming in the clouds of heaven." Then Caiaphas rent his garments and exclaimed, "He hath spoken blasphemy; what further need have we of witnesses? behold, now ye have heard his blasphemy" (Matthew 26:63-65). It was contrary to the law for the high priest to rend his garments, and the moment he did that the priesthood passed away from Israel. But Jesus did not answer Caiaphas until he put Him on oath. He knew there was no honesty, no desire to know what was true, but He gave to Pilate the benefit of the doubt.

Pilate seemed to be sincere, it seemed as though he would really like to know, and so Jesus explained very carefully, and then closed with the challenging word: "Every one that is of the truth heareth my voice." Let me bring that home to you. "Every one that is of the truth heareth my voice." Do not say to me, do not say to the Spirit of God, do not say to your own soul, "I cannot believe that Jesus Christ is the Son of God; I cannot believe that Jesus Christ is the rightful head of a spiritual kingdom." To say that implies that you are not an honest man or woman, for Jesus Christ says, "Every one that is of the truth heareth my voice." If you are determined to be true, if you are determined to be real, if you mean to be honest to the deepest convictions of your own soul, you will know who He is. He says elsewhere, "If any man will do his will, he shall know of the doctrine, whether it be of God, or whether I speak of myself" (John 7:17). If a man says, "I would like to believe, but some way I cannot," the reason is not difficult to find. If you say you would like to believe that Jesus Christ is the Son of God, but you cannot, if you would like to believe that the Bible is truly the Word of God but you cannot, it is because you are living in some sin that the Bible condemns. That is why you cannot believe.

When someone said to Sir Isaac Newton, "I would like to believe but cannot," he said, "Sometimes in my absent-mindedness I come into my study and try to light my candle without taking the snuffer off, and of course I cannot light it, but when the snuffer is off, then I can light the candle." The snuffer is a hidden sin in your life from which you do not want to be delivered. If you honestly desire to be delivered from all iniquity, depend upon it you will have no trouble believing the gospel message if you come to God in repentance, acknowledging your guilt. "Every one that is of the truth heareth my voice."' This was a challenge to Pilate. He stopped a moment, looked at the prisoner before him, and then asked the question in a weary kind of voice, "What is truth?" As much as to say, "Who can know what truth is?" Lord Bacon wrote:

> "What is truth?" said jesting Pilate
> And waited not for an answer.

Truth incarnate stood before him, yet Pilate had no eyes to see because he was blinded by worldly ambition.

If Pilate had said, "What is it? Explain it, make it clear to me," Jesus would have unfolded the truth to him, but he put the question, "What is truth?" and turned away. Yet he was convinced that Jesus was not guilty of any crime against the government. He said to the people, "I find in him no fault at all" (John 18:38). And then as they accused Him vehemently, somebody mentioned the fact that He was a Galilean, and Pilate immediately took it up and said, "Is He from Galilee? Well, Herod is the tetrarch of Galilee and is here at the present time. I will let him pass upon the case" (Luke 23:6-7). This seemed to Pilate a convenient way of getting out of taking a definite stand for or against the Lord Jesus Christ. We know what happened when Jesus went to Herod. Herod, hard and cruel, with a conscience seared as with a hot iron, allowed those soldiers of his to mock the blessed Christ of God, and then sent Him again to Pilate. And Pilate said to himself, "How shall I get out of this? Here is Jesus; I must do something about Him. I do not believe He is guilty, but these Jews insist that He is. How can I get out of it?" Then he remembered that in order to curry favor with the Jews, an edict had been pronounced that at the Passover time the Roman government would set free one Jewish prisoner, whomsoever the Jews desired.

At that time there was a notable Jewish robber, Barabbas by name, in prison. Barabbas means, "son of the father." Jesus was the true "Son of the Father." Pilate said, "I am going to give you the opportunity of setting a prisoner free; you shall enjoy the prerogative and say who shall be free." "Will ye therefore that I release unto you the King of the Jews?" But they all cried out, "Not this man, but Barabbas." Though Barabbas was a patriot he was a robber and murderer. Pilate hesitated and thought, "They have put me in a tight place, whatever shall I do now? If I let Barabbas go free, I do not know what to do with Jesus."

Just then a page came in and attracted his attention. He had come with a note for Pilate. It was a message from his own wife and it said, "Have thou nothing to do with that just man: for I have suffered many things this day in a dream because of him" (Matthew 27:19). It was probably signed by her. We know her name, for it has come down in history. Her name was

Claudia Procula. The early Christians said she died a Christian. As Pilate looked at that his hand trembled. He loved his wife so tenderly and now she was pleading for the life of this prisoner and the people were still crying, "Barabbas! Barabbas! Release unto us Barabbas."

Pilate stood before them and presented Jesus as he said, "Behold the man!" Surely as they gaze upon Him, as they look upon that innocent and yet marred face, their hard hearts will be softened; they will realize that He is no criminal. But they cried out the more vehemently, "Not this man, but Barabbas," and then he put the question that has come ringing down the ages, the question that comes to every man or woman today, "What shall I do then with Jesus which is called Christ?" "If I use the prerogative of releasing one man and that one is Barabbas, what shall I do with this man?" That is the question that you must decide—what will you do with Jesus?

> "What will you do with Jesus?"
> The call comes low and sweet,
> As tenderly He bids you
> Your burdens lay at His feet.
>
> O soul, so sad and weary,
> That sweet voice pleads with thee,
> Then what will you do with Jesus?
> Oh, what shall the answer be?

There was no hesitation on their part. Stirred up by the chief priests they cried with one voice, "Crucify him! Crucify him!" Pilate stood there again in perplexity. He went back to the judgment seat and summoned Jesus once more and put the question, "Whence art thou?" (John 19:9) In other words, "Where do you come from, and what is your origin? You are different from other men; who are you really? Whose case is it upon which I am called to pronounce judgment today?" But Jesus gave him no answer. It was evident that Pilate was no longer the honest inquirer. He was determined to placate the Jews and yet hold favor with Caesar, no matter what it might mean. However, he would like to release Jesus. But there was no reply. And Pilate said, "Speakest thou not unto me? Knowest thou not that I have power to crucify thee, and have power to release thee?" In other words, "Don't you know that the issues of life and death are in my hands?" Then Jesus spoke, and He put the judge in the place of the prisoner when He said: "Thou couldest have no power at all against me, except it were given thee from above; therefore he that delivered me unto thee hath the greater sin." Now Pilate used every effort in his power to move the hearts of these people to pity, to sympathy, but the answer comes: "If thou let this man go, thou art not Caesar's friend: whosoever maketh himself a king speaketh against Caesar." There is an accusation at last! This man is setting himself up as a king in rebellion against Caesar, and now, Pontius Pilate, if you let Him go, we will send the charge to Rome that we found this man teaching sedition, and that instead of pronouncing sentence upon Him you let Him go free, and you will lose your position!

The governor had taken a basin of water and ostentatiously washed his hands in it, saying, "I am innocent of the blood of this just person" (Matthew 27:24). He brought Jesus forth once more with a crown of thorns pressed upon His brow and said, "Behold your King!" but again they cried, "Away with him! Away with him! Crucify him!" Pilate asked but one more question, "Shall I crucify your King?" Again they exclaimed, "We have no king but Caesar." And weary with the struggle, Pilate gave up. What difference does it make? He will sacrifice one almost unknown Galilean Jew and save his own good name with Caesar; so he delivered Jesus to be crucified and they took Him and led Him away.

Pilate had every opportunity to be saved, but that overweening sin of ambition, that desire to be thought well of by Caesar, that desire to be looked up to by the people, was too much for him. He gave Jesus to the death of the cross in order to save himself from shame, and what was the result? The centuries since have fixed upon him eternal infamy, "Crucified under Pontius Pilate." All his life long he had the memory of this miscarriage of judgment resting in his mind and on his life. The dreadful thing was upon his conscience, and when some four or five years later he went out into eternity as a suicide, he went to face forever the charge, "Jesus was crucified under Pontius Pilate." He is facing it today and he shall face it for all eternity. This man had the opportunity of siding with Christ in the hour of the Savior's great distress, but he delivered Jesus to the will of the people.

My friend, I bring the question home to you, "What will you do with Jesus which is called Christ?" Jesus is on trial here today; the Spirit of God is saying to you, "What are you going to do with Him?" You must do one of two things. Will you accept Him as your Savior, own Him as Lord, or will you reject and spurn Him? You may say, "But I am not going to do anything about it now. I am going to think it through." The very fact that you do not decide to receive Him as Savior and Lord is your decision to reject Him, at least at the present moment. Pontius Pilate tried to be neutral and found that it was an impossibility. You cannot be neutral. It is not enough to say that you recognize in Him the greatest and best of the sons of men; it is not enough to admit that no other ever taught as Jesus taught; it must be more than that. You must see in Him the sinner's Savior; you must come to Him in all your guilt and trust Him for yourself.

A few years ago a Jewish merchant died. He had a Christian friend who was in the same business, and they would often without any prejudice talk of the claims of Jesus Christ. The

Jewish merchant had never accepted Christ as Savior, and when he was dying his family did not want to allow any Gentile to get near him; but the Christian associate was eager to see him, and they felt that they could not refuse him because he had been a close friend. But they said, "You must not talk religion to him, you must not excite him." He went in and sat for a moment by the bedside, touched the hand of his friend, and then knelt by the bed and silently lifted his heart to God. Soon there was a movement on the bed. The old man opened his eyes, tried to sit up, lifted his hand, and struggling to speak, said, "Not Barabbas, but this Man," and he fell back dead. Do you see what he had done? He had reversed the sentence of his nation. His nation had said, "Not this Man, but Barabbas," but he said, "Not Barabbas, but this Man."

What are you saying? Do you prefer the robbers of earth, those who would rob you of everything good and pure and holy? Or will you definitely decide to take Jesus Christ to be your own personal Savior? "What shall I do with Jesus which is called Christ?" Pontius Pilate made a fearful mistake which is now irrevocable. It can never be changed; never can he get away from that awful sentence of the Creed, "Crucified under Pontius Pilate."

O my friend, be careful that you make not the same mistake by rejecting Christ. Will you receive Him? Will you take Him as your Savior? "Whosoever therefore shall confess me before men, him will I confess also before my Father which is in heaven" (Matthew 10:32). Will you make this good confession? Will you take Jesus Christ as your personal Savior? The very moment you come to the place where you are ready to receive Him, that moment He receives you. "Him that cometh unto me I will in no wise cast out." Never mind what sin has been holding you back. Do you desire to be saved from it? Then come to Him, come to Jesus. "Thou shalt call his name Jesus, for he shall save his people from their sins."

Chapter Ten

The Folly of Procrastination

When I have a convenient season I will call for thee.
(Acts 24:25)

I am not going to occupy you with the story of Felix, his duplicity, his perfidy, and his folly in deferring the question of salvation until for him, I fear, it was forever too late. For as you know, what little history records concerning him suggests that he lived and died in his sins. But I want you to consider with me the foolishness of following his example in saying, not so much perhaps to a servant of God, but to the Holy Spirit of God, what he said to the apostle Paul, "When I have a convenient season I will call for thee."

I am addressing myself, I presume, to an audience composed largely of Christians, yet I am sure there are many here tonight who are still without the saving knowledge of Christ. I take it for granted you intend to become a Christian some day. You have not thought of spending all your life in rebellion against God and going out into eternity an impenitent sinner to be lost forever. You have said to yourself over and over again, "Some day I must settle this question, and settle it in the right way. Some day I must yield to the voice of God; some day I must accept Christ's gracious invitation." But you have added, "Not now. When I have a convenient season, a more convenient season, I will take this matter up and give it my serious attention."

Let me earnestly inquire, When do you think that more convenient season will arrive? When do you think it will be easier to face your sins in the presence of God, to confess them, to turn to God in definite repentance, and to accept the Lord Jesus Christ by faith as your Savior, than it would be now?

Will it be a more convenient season, a better time to go into this matter, when perchance you are stricken down by illness and find yourself lying helplessly on a sick bed? Is this your idea of a convenient season? When you can no longer rush around as you do now, but when on a bed, racked by pain and weakened by disease, you lie in a quiet room, or perhaps in a hospital ward, with plenty of time to think, and to weigh the great questions of time and eternity? Are you so sure this will be a more convenient season? Do you think it more likely that you will be in a better condition to take up such tremendous issues when weak and sick and perhaps tormented by anxiety as to the final outcome? During the years in which I have sought to preach the gospel of Christ, I have sat by thousands of sick beds. I have been sent again and again by anxious relatives who have said to me something like this, "This son (this husband, this wife, this daughter, or whatever else the relationship may be) is very ill and we fear has never turned to Christ. Will you not come to see if you could help such an one to a definite decision?" And so often I have gone in and the nurse has said, "Be careful; do not say anything that would excite the patient," or, "The doctor has warned against anything that might make the sick one think that death is near," and I have felt so handicapped as I have tried to speak of Christ and the soul's great need. But in so many instances the brain has been so overwrought or the nervous system so upset that I could only get in a few words, and then after reading some passages from God's blessed Book kneel in prayer, and commit the sick one to Christ. I am afraid that sometimes I have actually prayed rather for the edification, as I hoped, of the patient, than that my words might reach the ears of God, that is, hoping that indirectly some expressions used in the prayer might be carried by the Spirit of God home to the heart of the one who lay there so restless or perhaps so lethargic; and over and over again, when the end has come there has been no assurance whatever that the Word has found lodgment in the soul or that the sinner was saved.

My friend, a sickbed is a poor place upon which to settle the question of one's relationship to God. Today while you are strong and well, while the eye is clear and bright, and the breath comes regularly, and the pulse beats in an orderly way, it is the time to attend to the question of your soul's salvation. Do not, I beg of you, think of a sickbed as affording a more convenient season.

Then again in this rushing work-a-day age when there seems so little time for quiet meditation, are you saying to yourself, "When I can take life more leisurely, when I do not have so much to occupy me, perhaps when I have made my fortune and can retire from business, that will be a more convenient season, and then I will attend to the matter of getting right with God"? But have you ever reflected how many people there are who never attain to this period of leisure? Do you realize that the great majority of us are so situated that we have to work on and on saving very little; and then perhaps by some unexpected change of condition, lose all that we have saved, and so struggle for bread and butter right up to the last, until eventually the poor overwrought heart suddenly stops and we go out to meet God. Oh, what a solemn thing if one is thus called to meet Him unprepared! You have,

> Room for pleasure, room for business,
> But for Christ the crucified,
> Not a place that He can enter
> In the heart for which He died.

You remember the other verse of that old gospel hymn:

> Have you any time for Jesus,
> As in grace He calls again?
> Oh, today is time accepted,
> Tomorrow He may call in vain.

While you are waiting for a time of greater leisure, when as you fancy you may with less distraction take up and settle the solemn problems that have to do with your eternal welfare, will you not remember that it is given to very few indeed to ever reach such a desirable state in life? Surely then the only wise thing is to heed the call of God now.

Jesus called Peter from a busy fisherman's life. He called Matthew from the tax collector's office where he was doubtless literally overwhelmed with work. He stopped Saul of Tarsus in the midst of a rushing career, and all found salvation through heeding His Word. You do not need more leisure in order to inquire more particularly in regard to these things. The gospel is so plain, the invitation is so clear, the message is so simple, you have but to lift your heart in the midst of all the rushing things of life and look to Jesus in faith, to be eternally saved.

> Room and time now give to Jesus,
> Soon will pass God's day of grace;
> Soon thy heart be cold and silent,
> And thy Saviour's pleading cease.

Are there others who saying, perhaps not with the lips but at least in their hearts, "Go Thy way for this time. When I am old, I will send for Thee"? Are you cherishing the hope that in old age if you ever attain to it, you will be better prepared to come to Christ than you are in your youth or in middle life?

Do you realize that very few old people who have lived all their lives in sin ever turn to Christ at last? Do you remember that the Holy Scripture speaks of the heart being hardened by the deceitfulness of sin? Do you recall that there is such a thing as the conscience becoming seared as with a hot iron, so that it ceases to register? You have often heard the expression, "He, or she, is gospel-hardened," and it sets forth a condition to which many, alas, attain. There are people all over Christendom who have heard the gospel so many times that it ceases to move them in the slightest degree. Pharaoh hardened his heart against God so often that at last we read, "the Lord hardened Pharaoh's heart" (Exodus 10:20). How did He harden it? Simply by the repeated declarations of His will to which Pharaoh refused to give heed. The sun which softens the wax hardens the clay, and the same gospel message which melts the tender heart of an exercised youth, will make no impression whatever, perchance, upon the hard heart of an aged sinner.

I will never forget listening night after night to Dwight L. Moody in the old Hazzard's Pavilion, Los Angeles, when I was but a lad of twelve. I could not get a seat the first night I went, the place was so full, so I climbed out on one of the steel girders reaching from the top gallery supported from the roof, and there I lay looking down upon the great throng, watching the sturdily built matter-of-fact, businesslike man, who had been advertised as the renowned evangelist, Moody. I was greatly impressed by his intensity, and many a time as I lay there, I said in my heart, "Oh, how glad I would be if I could some day reach great throngs of people with the gospel in the way that man is doing." I remember so well one night Mr. Moody asked all who were sure they were converted to stand on their feet. He kept them standing while the ushers gave an estimate of the number who had risen. They were reported to be between five and six thousand. Then Mr. Moody asked all who had come to Christ before they were fifteen years of age to sit down. To my amazement, fully two-thirds of that great throng dropped to their seats. Then he said, "All who became Christians before you were twenty, sit down." Less than one-half of those left standing remained on their feet. Then he requested all who were saved under thirty to sit down, and another great company took their seats. So it went on, those under forty, under fifty, and by that time there were perhaps not twenty people still standing. It was one of the most striking testimonies I have ever seen of the fact that the great majority of people are saved in early youth, and very few indeed ever turn to God after they have passed the half-century mark. What stupendous folly then for any one with whom the Spirit is now pleading to say, "When I get old, it will be a more convenient season. Let me alone now, Holy Spirit of God; come back to me when my hair is white, my step is infirm, my eyes are dim, and my nerves shattered, and my whole body has become decrepit and infirm."

Or are there some here who are saying, "When I feel different, then I will come"? You think the present is not a propitious season because you are not overwhelmed with emotions. But on some future occasion when your feelings are more deeply stirred, when perhaps you imagine yourself to be better than you are now, or more interested in spiritual things, then you will come to Christ and close with His offer of mercy. Have you noticed that God nowhere asks you to feel different before you come to Jesus? Everywhere the Scripture insists on immediate response to the call of God irrespective of frames or feelings. It is not necessary that you go through some great emotional experience in order to trust in Christ. You remember the old hymn:

> Let not conscience make you linger,
>   Nor of fitness fondly dream;
> All the fitness Christ requireth

> Is to feel your need of Him.
> This He gives you,
> Tis the Spirit's rising beam.
>
> Come, ye weary, heavy laden,
> Bruised and ruined by the fall;
> If you tarry 'till you're better,
> You will never come at all;
> Not the righteous—sinners Jesus came to call.

You do not have to improve yourself before coming to Christ. He is not calling you to cleanse your own heart from its sinfulness or to break off evil habits that have bound you. You are not asked to help Him save you, but He offers to take you just as you are, and save you fully and completely by His own almighty power.

And now I would ask you to consider the divine answer to your suggestion that you wait for a more convenient season. In 2 Corinthians 6:2 the Holy Spirit has said, "Behold, now is the accepted time, behold, now is the day of salvation." And in Hebrews 3:15 we read, "Today, if you will hear his voice, harden not your hearts." Why should you thus attempt to defer the settlement of your soul's salvation when God is so ready to save you now?

Consider four things which I want to press upon you briefly in closing.

1. Remember no better time will ever come. No matter if you live to a vigorous old age, you will never have a better opportunity to close with Christ than you have now, and it is questionable if you will ever be more ready to be saved. In the meantime, even supposing you come after sixty or seventy years of living in sin, you will have lost just that much joy and peace which you might have had by being saved earlier.

2. This is of great importance. You will never have fewer sins

to account for than you have tonight. Do not say, "I am not a great sinner". What do you mean by that? If you are still rejecting Christ, you are guilty of the worst sin any one can possibly commit, for nothing can exceed in guilt the spurning of God's own blessed Son. But take the question of actual violations of His holy law. Every day that you live, you are adding to the number of your transgressions. Suppose that you only commit three sins a day, one in thought, one in word, and one in deed; that would be in round numbers 1,000 sins a year, and you are perchance 20, 30, 40, 50 years of age. Then you are guilty of 20, 30, 40, 50,000 sins already, and every day you live you are adding to the number. Is it not the greatest folly to go on increasing your guilt while hoping for a more convenient season to be cleansed therefrom? But who is there who has only committed three sins a day? Is it not a dreadful fact that the record is far greater than that, and that you now stand guilty before God of untold myriad of sins for which no other atonement is possible than that which was made by Christ upon the cross? Why not then trust at once in Him who died and have the blessed assurance that all your sins are forever cast into the sea of God's forgetfulness?

3. In the third place, consider, God will never be more ready to save you than He is now. He has manifested His love to the fullest extent in sending His only begotten Son to be the propitiation for our sins. He has given His Holy Spirit to convince of sin, righteousness, and judgment. He has sent His messengers out into all the world with the gospel proclamation. Everywhere they go they are instructed to cry, "All things are ready! Come!" Do you not see that you are insulting God when you coldly turn away and say, "I intend to accept the invitation some day but not now. When I have a convenient season, I will call for Thee."

4. Lastly, let me affectionately remind you that the gospel will never be more efficacious to bring peace to your weary

heart than now. The blood of Christ will never avail to any greater extent than at this present moment to cleanse your conscience from every stain of sin and make you perfectly fit for the presence of God. The work of the cross is finished. There is nothing to be added to what Christ has done. God calls upon you to believe the message and to bow in thanksgiving at the Savior's feet. Will you not do this now while our hearts are lifted up to Him in earnest prayer for all in His presence who are still unsaved?

CHAPTER ELEVEN

Prophecy

An Outstanding Proof of the Inspiration of the Bible

The prophecy came not in old time by the will of man: but holy men of God spake as they were moved by the Holy Ghost.

(2 PETER 1:21)

I wonder how many of you have ever stopped to consider the fact that the Bible is the only Book of prophecy in all the world. We know there are books that many regard as sacred literature, and sometimes scholars who specialize in the study of comparative religions are inclined to put these so-called sacred books on a level with the Bible, the Word of the living God. However you can take all these other books and pile them up on one side and put the Bible alone on the other, and the Bible is the only one that is marked out as divine by the fact that it contains hundreds of prophecies uttered thousands of years ago, most of which have been fulfilled to the letter. Others are being fulfilled at the present moment, so we may feel certain that those which have not yet come to fruition will do so eventually.

This was brought to my attention a good many years ago, at a time when as a young Christian I needed it very much. I was about fifteen years of age and had only been converted a few months, and I was eager to learn everything I could about the

Bible. I noticed a course of lectures on "The Bible as Literature" advertised in the papers. I arranged to attend some of the meetings and hear at least a few of the addresses. But when I went the first night I found that they were not at all what I had hoped. The lecturer, though cultured and eloquent, was really an agnostic and did not believe in the Bible as a message from Heaven. He spoke fluently of its literary appeal and all that, and I think maybe I learned a little bit from him along those lines, but he made it very evident that he considered it absurd to accept the idea that the Bible was divinely inspired.

One thing he said that night troubled me very much. As nearly as I can now recall, he spoke like this: "Do you believe the Bible to be the very Word of God? If so, have you ever stopped to inquire why you hold that belief?" Then, after an impressive pause, he continued: "I will tell you why you believe it. It is simply because your parents did so before you. They taught you that the Bible was the Word of God, and you accepted their teaching without taking the trouble to investigate for yourselves. If you had been born into a Hindu family, you would believe in the Vedic scriptures just as you now believe in the Bible. If you had been born into a Buddhist family, you would accept the teachings of Buddha and the other Buddhist writings as you now accept the teachings of Moses and Jesus and the other Biblical writers. If you had been born into a Parsee family, the Zend Avesta would be to you just what the Bible is to you now. If you had been born into a Mohammedan family, you would believe in the Koran as you now believe in the Bible. If you had been born into a Taoist, or a Confucian Chinese family, the writings of Lao Tsze or the philosophy of Confucius would have meant to you just exactly what the Bible does."

I had never heard anyone put it like that before and as a young convert it troubled me very much. I asked myself, "Is it true that after all I have a second-hand faith? Is it a fact that I am a Christian by profession simply because my parents were?

Is my faith in the Bible just the same as the faith of all those other people in their sacred books?" Then I determined to investigate those books and see for myself whether they were worthy to be put on a level with the Bible.

I remember well going up to the city library and saying to the lady at the desk, "I would like to see all the different Bibles of the world." She looked at me, smiled, and said, "My dear boy, there is only one Bible." She was a very wise woman. "But," I replied, "what I mean is I want to see the books that the people of other religions put in place of the Bible—their sacred books." She led me to a certain alcove in the library, and there on a long ten-foot shelf were the great volumes containing translations of nearly all of the sacred books of the world, as prepared by Dr. Max Muller of Oxford and his associates. I read over the titles of perhaps thirty-eight of these books, so large that they resembled a file of old encyclopedias, though the paper was thick and the printing large. I said, "These are what I want." The librarian asked with a smile, "Do you want to take them all with you?" "No," I replied, "but I have three cards here, one in my mother's name, one in my brother's name and one in my own. I would like to take three of them out, and when I bring them back I will take the next three, and so on until I finish them." I think she was quite amused, but I was in dead earnest. Off I went with my three great books, all I could carry, and that very night I began to read them. It took me many weeks before I had finished the last of the set, but when I had gone through them all, ten feet of religion without the cross, I found I had learned several things, and these things have been of value to me throughout all the rest of my life.

In the first place, I found that I had the wrong idea about some of the great ethnic religions. I had supposed there was nothing good in them whatsoever, but I discovered that there were many very fine moral and religious sentiments, often expressed very beautifully. It was easy to see that some of these writers had a certain measure of moral and spiritual illumination, but as a rule the truths they enunciated were just like so many rare gems in the midst of a mass of worthless rubbish.

But, in the second place, it began to dawn upon me that I had not found in all those thirty-eight volumes one moral or spiritual truth which I did not have in the Bible already. Now this is a remarkable thing: the Bible is not a very large book and yet—think of it!—in all that great mass of literature I could not find one positively true statement having to do with the moral or spiritual life that could add anything to the Bible. While I am on that, let me say another thing: many years have rolled by since the time I waded through those pagan books; but in all these additional years I have never found in any literature, a solitary moral or spiritual truth that is not in my Bible. I commend that statement to you for your careful consideration.

But now the third thing that made a tremendous impression on me at the time, and which has meant much to me during all the years, is this: in all those great volumes there was not one definite prophetic statement that had ever been fulfilled. There were attempts at prophecy, but nothing to compare with the prophecy of the Bible, and though I was only fifteen years of age I saw then how definitely the Bible stands by itself as the only book of prophecy in the world. Then I could say, "The lecturer is wrong; I do not believe the Bible simply because my parents believed it and taught me that it was the Word of God. I thank God that in His infinite lovingkindness He permitted me to be born in a Christian home, and I praise Him for the teaching of godly parents, but I can say without any hesitation, 'I believe this Book because I cannot do otherwise. It carries its own credentials with it. The prophetic seal proves it to be the Word of God.'"

There are nine chapters in the book of the prophet Isaiah in which God Himself stresses this view of things. In this section God takes up the question of idolatry with His people. They had turned from Him, many of them, to the various idolatrous systems of the heathen around about them, and in these chapters we have Jehovah's controversy with idols. There are many very striking things set forth in a most graphic manner. Notice Isaiah's description of the making of an idol: "To whom then will ye liken God? or what likeness will ye compare unto him? The workman melteth a graven image, and the goldsmith spreadeth it over with gold, and casteth silver chains. He that is so impoverished that he hath no oblation chooseth a tree that will not rot; he seeketh unto him a cunning workman to prepare a graven image, that shall not be moved" (Isaiah 40:18-20).

Do you get the irony of that? A God that cannot walk. Then in vivid contrast, "Have ye not known? have ye not heard? hath it not been told you from the beginning? have ye not understood from the foundations of the earth? It is he that sitteth upon the circle of the earth, and the inhabitants thereof are as grasshoppers; that stretcheth out the heavens as a curtain, and spreadeth them out as a tent to dwell in; That bringeth the princes to nothing; he maketh the judges of the earth as vanity" (Isaiah 40:21-23). To whom will you liken Him? In the sublimest way, again and again he comes back to this, the greatness and the majesty of the true God.

In this section, over and over again God challenges the representatives of all the different pagan religions, the priests and prophets of these heathen systems, to prove the divinity of their religions by prophecy. Notice Isaiah 41:21-24: "Produce your cause, saith the Lord; bring forth your strong reasons, saith the King of Jacob. Let them bring them forth, and shew us what shall happen: let them shew the former things, what they be, that we may consider them, and know the latter end of them; or declare us things for to come. Shew the things that are to come hereafter, that we may know that ye are gods: yea, do good, or do evil, that we may be dismayed, and behold it together. Behold, ye are of nothing, and your work of nought." You see it is a challenge, as though He says, "If there is anything supernatural about your religion, if there is any divine power back of your idols, demonstrate it by prophecy. Show us things to come or go back into the past and tell us how things came to be. Explain the mystery of the creation and make clear to us its end." They could not do it.

Then look at Isaiah 43:9-10: "Let all the nations be gathered together, and let the people be assembled: who among them can declare this, and shew us former things? Let them bring forth their witnesses, that they may be justified: or let them hear, and say, It is truth.[And to Israel He said] Ye are my witnesses, saith the Lord, and my servant whom I have chosen: that ye may know and believe me, and understand that I am he: before me there was no God formed, neither shall there be after me." That is, the history of Israel bears witness to the reality of the God of Israel, to His personality and intelligence. And then the prophet says, as it were, "The proof that I am telling you the truth is that God is speaking through me. Go down through the centuries, and after I tell you of things to come, and they take place, you will have proof of this. Ye (the nation of Israel) are my witnesses." It makes no difference whether the people of Israel are obedient or disobedient, whether they are in the land of Palestine or scattered among the nations; wherever they are and whatever they are doing, the history of this people is proof that God is the living God.

Some of the prophecies which this book contains have been history for thirty-five hundred years. Beginning with Moses on the plains of Moab, he there foretold the history of the people ahead of time, and thirty-five centuries have shown the fulfillment of the prophecy. Israel has been acting exactly as God said they would, and the events that have taken place as Moses predicted have proven His foreknowledge.

You have often heard the story of Frederick the Great, with which almost every lecturer on the Jews begins his address. Frederick the Great had become skeptical and unbelieving, largely through the agnostic and scornful views of Voltaire, that man so brilliant and witty, trained for a Catholic priest, who turned in disgust from the superstition and the sham of it all, rejecting all belief or faith in it. Sometimes I feel sorry for Voltaire, for I realize that in his younger days he was not to be blamed for a great many things he said, for he was really a victim of circumstances. We think of his blasphemous expression, "Crush the wretch!" and then of his speech when someone mentioned the name of Jesus, "I pray you, let me never hear the name of that Man again." But he did not really know the Son of God. The Jesus he had in mind was the Jesus of the false priests of the superstitious Church of Rome. Voltaire hated the religion he had found in the Roman system, and he instilled his doubts into the mind of Frederick. One day the Prussian turned to one of the chaplains and said, "If your Bible is really true, it ought to be capable of very brief proof. So many times when I have asked for proof of the inspiration of the Bible, I have been handed some great and learned tome that I have neither time nor inclination to read, some volume on the evidence of Christianity that I could never wade through. If your Bible really is from Heaven, give me the proof of it in one word." And the good man replied, "Israel, your Majesty." Frederick was silent.

Israel is the proof that the Bible is the Word of the living God. It is unthinkable that the history of any nation should be forecast as the history of Israel was, for thirty-five hundred years in advance, if this Book is not from God.

Then to pass on—for I want you to note the challenging way in which the Lord continues to put this—read Isaiah 44:7: "And who, as I, shall call, and shall declare it, and set it in order for me, since I appointed the ancient people? and the things that are coming, and shall come, let them shew unto them." Someone has well said, "All history is His story." God has foreknown and foretold all in His Book, and the unfolding of history is simply but the proof of prophecy, and that is the stand that God Himself takes here.

Then turn to Isaiah 45:11: "Thus saith the Lord, the Holy One of Israel, and his Maker, Ask me of things to come concerning my sons, and concerning the work of my hands command ye me." And Isaiah 46:9-10: "Remember the former things of old: for I am God, and there is none else; I am God, and there is none like me, Declaring the end from the beginning, and from ancient times the things that are not yet done, saying, My counsel shall stand, and I will do all my pleasure."

Then Isaiah 48:3: "I have declared the former things from the beginning; and they went forth out of my mouth, and I shewed them; I did them suddenly, and they came to pass."

I have taken several verses from Isaiah 40–48 to lead you to carefully read the entire section and get the argument, that the Spirit of God may prepare you for the better refutation of every false religious system. You have here that which will help you when dealing with unbelievers. One of the very best ways to deal with people who say they do not believe the Bible is to ask them, "How do you explain the prophetic element in the Scriptures?"

Generally you will be answered in one of two ways: Either he will say, "I don't believe there is any prophecy in the Bible," or, "I don't know anything about it." If he says he does not believe there is prophecy in the Bible, you get so well acquainted with your Bible that you can turn to some direct prophecy and ask him to explain it. If he says he doesn't know anything about it, try to get him to go with you into a careful study of prophecy and its fulfillment. I like the method that John Urquhart uses in his "The Wonders of Prophecy." This is the principle that he lays down for the question of proof. We will study some of the great prophecies of the Bible, and then we will turn to history to see how they were fulfilled. We will just put out of our minds all the prophecies that are found in one part of the Bible and the story of their fulfillment in another. There are a great many such prophecies. For instance, you might read Isaiah 53, and then turn to the New Testament and follow the fulfillment out for yourself. Or for the Babylonian captivity, read the prophecies in Leviticus and Isaiah and Jeremiah, and then turn to the book of Daniel and others, and see how they were fulfilled. But many prophecies of Scripture were not fulfilled when the last book of the Bible was written. It has been in the centuries since that they have come to pass, and that with the utmost particularity, exactly as predicted. This is true of the great prophecies relating to Edom, to Tyre, to Egypt and other nations. It is pre-eminently true when the experiences of the Jews for the past eighteen hundred years are depicted. Until one has carefully studied along these lines, he has no right to reject the Bible; and every one who honestly investigates in this way must, it seems to me, realize that "All Scripture is God-breathed."

An honest person, with ordinary intelligence, who really desires to know whether the Bible is true, will soon realize that it is impossible—no, absolutely unthinkable—that prophecy and history should so perfectly dovetail into each other if a divine mind had not given to the prophet the foresight to show things yet to come. And the God who inspired the Biblical writers is the God who gave His Son to redeem lost men.

Chapter Twelve

"Where Is the Promise of His Coming?"

This second epistle, beloved, I now write unto you; in both which I stir up your pure minds by way of remembrance: That ye may be mindful of the words which were spoken before by the holy prophets, and of the commandment of us the apostles of the Lord and Saviour: Knowing this first, that there shall come in the last days scoffers, walking after their own lusts, And saying, Where is the promise of his coming? for since the fathers fell asleep, all things continue as they were from the beginning of the creation. For this they willingly are ignorant of, that by the word of God the heavens were of old, and the earth standing out of the water and in the water: Whereby the world that then was, being overflowed with water, perished: But the heavens and the earth, which are now, by the same word are kept in store, reserved unto fire against the day of judgment and perdition of ungodly men. But, beloved, be not ignorant of this one thing, that one day is with the Lord as a thousand years, and a thousand years as one day. The Lord is not slack concerning his promise, as some men count slackness; but is longsuffering to usward, not willing that any should perish, but that all should come to repentance.

(2 Peter 3:1-9)

In asking you to consider with me the promise of the return of our blessed Lord, I realize that I am touching on a subject which in many quarters is taboo. Nor am I surprised that there are actually ministers who look askance at the theme of the Lord's second coming because, I readily admit, there has been a great deal of fanatical, foolish, and utterly unscriptural teaching linked with this blessed hope. But what doctrine is there of which Scripture treats that men have not misused and misrepresented? Is this then a valid reason why those who are sound in the faith and seek to be guided by the Word of God alone should refrain from endeavoring to present the truth?

Years ago I had my attention directed to the fact that one verse in every twenty-five in the New Testament deals with the second coming of the Lord. I said to myself, "Then hereafter I must be sure that at least one sermon in every twenty-five has to do with this theme." I should think that would be about the right proportion, would not you? But I found that people were so interested in the subject and so helped by it, and its influence was so manifestly for good that I soon began doubling up, and possibly now I preach on it even more frequently than that. But I have no apologies to make for so doing, for, you see, I am trying to make up for so many of my brethren who never preach on it at all!

Surely we are living in the days when men are doing exactly as the Holy Spirit through Peter declared they would do. How often we hear the sneering question, "Where is the promise of his coming?" and we are reminded that for hundreds of years enthusiasts have spoken fervently of the imminent return of Christ, and yet the promise is still unfulfilled, and we are pointed to the supposed facts that things continue as they were, with no more evidence in our day of our Savior's near return than in years gone by.

But what I want to try to show you now is that all things do not continue as they were. We are living in times of flux and change. Wherever we look we see evidences that conditions are now prevailing such as Scripture plainly declares would characterize the last days of the church dispensation immediately preceding the second advent.

For your convenience I want to divide these signs into three groups in accordance with the admonition given to the Corinthians, "give none offense, neither to the Jews, nor to the Gentiles, nor to the church of God" (1 Corinthians 10:32). We are told in Ecclesiastes 4:12 that "a threefold cord is not quickly broken." As we consider prevailing conditions among these three groups, we shall see, I think, that we have here such a threefold cord of testimony indicating the nearness of our hope.

A great deal of prophetic Scripture has to do with the Jew whom someone has called "God's great timepiece." What marvelous events have taken place in connection with these people during the past generation! The rise of the Zionist Movement, the driving of the Turk out of Palestine, the Balfour Declaration opening their ancient patrimony to the Jewish people; the remarkable return to Palestine of approximately 200,000 Jews within the last few years; and the amazing developments now going on in that ancient country, all of these things tell us that the fig tree is beginning to bud, that Jewish national spirit has been revived, and an era of preparation for the coming of the King has dawned. All this is in accordance with the prophetic Word. It is evident from a careful study of the Scriptures, that in the last days the Jews are to be back in their own land, still in unbelief at the very time when many remarkable Scriptures will be fulfilled in regard to their experiences immediately before Messiah appears. One could go into this in great detail did time permit, but I trust you are familiar enough with the Word of God along these lines, to see how different things are moving on in accord with divine prediction.

Then too there is a remarkable spiritual movement among the Jews that should be most encouraging. When our Lord returns a remnant will be found ready to greet Him and acknowledge Him as Savior and King. During the present age of grace this remnant of course is incorporated in the church, which is His body. One would naturally look for a great awakening among this people and a drawing of many to Christ before the dispensation ends, and this is exactly what we find. The heart of the Jew is turning toward Christ in a wonderful way. I cannot give exact statistics but I dare to say that more Jews have been brought to a saving knowledge of the Lord Jesus Christ in the last two decades than for possibly centuries before. The blindness is passing away because the fullness of the Gentiles will soon come in.

Then look abroad, and consider the changes taking place among the Gentile nations. Thrones and crowns have perished. Empires have been destroyed. Men have made all kinds of attempts to bring order out of chaos, but God's Word declares that there will be no lasting peace nor settled condition among the nations until Christ comes back. Think of those remarkable words in Ezekiel 21:26-27: "Thus saith the Lord God: Remove the diadem, and take off the crown: this shall not be the same; exalt him that is low, and abase him that is high. I will overturn, overturn, overturn, it: and it shall be no more, until he come whose right it is; and I will give it him." This process of overturning is very apparent today. Statesmen are at their wits' end. The hearts of men are failing them for fear and for looking after those things which are coming upon the earth.

Everywhere we see perplexity and unrest, but this is exactly what our Lord predicted as characteristic of the Gentile nations in the last days. It seems to me if one is familiar with prophecy he can see the great coalitions of the last times already forming. I dare not attempt to go into detail, but many of you will understand at once the references when I speak of the revived Roman Empire, the hosts of Gog and Magog, the king of the North and the king of the South, and the kings of the East, or the sun-rising. Remember when you study prophecy that, from God's standpoint, Jerusalem is always the center. The king of the South is Egypt, and what remarkable changes have taken place there; the king of the North is whatever power occupies Syria and what we know as Turkey in Asia, in the last days. Surely most portentous events are there taking place. The Roman coalition includes ten powers formed out of the old Roman Empire, all drawn together in a league, offensive and defensive, to endeavor to conserve the peace of the world, out of which will arise the great dictator of Revelation 13. Gog and Magog speak clearly, it seems to me, of Russia and her allies (scholars trace out the names of the various peoples now embraced in the league of the Soviet Republic), and others in sympathy with Bolshevism. The kings of the East would seem unquestionably to be the Oriental powers of the Far East, dominated by Japan, the Empire of the Rising Sun. These are the great coalitions that will participate in the final Armageddon, and surely it is not too much to say that the stage is already set for this last act of the great world drama. Strictly speaking, there will never be an actual battle of Armageddon, for when the hosts of the nations gather there for battle, the Lord Himself will interfere by descending in glory and scattering His foes.

Then we look at the church of God and ask ourselves, Could conditions in the professing church be more graphically depicted than we find them in the Epistles of the New Testament? Increasing apostasy, rejection of long-recognized truth, coldness and indifference to Christ on the one hand, and yet on the other an enlarged world vision, greater missionary activity than for many centuries, more eager desire after the Word of God and deeper spiritual life. These are the exact characteristics of the closing days of the church's testimony.

Now if we found conditions in Israel such as the prophets told us would be the case in the last days, but no such conditions yet prevailing among the Gentiles or in the professing church, we might be warranted in saying in measure at least with the skeptic, "My Lord delayeth His coming." Or if we found conditions among the nations such as the prophetic writings led us to expect, but nothing of the same character in Israel or the church, we might well ask, "Where is the promise of his coming?" On the other hand, if conditions in the church had developed as depicted prophetically, but there were no such alignments among the nations as the Word declares will be evidenced in the last days, nor yet any such movements in Israel as we have a right to look for, we might still hesitate regarding the proclamation of the very near advent of our Lord. But if, at one and the same time, we see all these three spheres characterized by the very things that the Holy Spirit through the prophets announced beforehand as evidences of the end times, our hearts may well be lifted up as we exclaim, "The coming of the Lord draweth nigh."

We are living in very solemn and serious times when every faithful minister of Christ should seek by every possible means to arouse people to the importance of getting right with God now, knowing that the time is short, and soon "the Master of the house will arise and shut the door" to those who now reject His grace. Let us remember our Lord's own words, "When these things begin to come to pass, then look up, and lift up your heads; for your redemption draweth nigh" (Luke 21:28).

> He is coming, coming, coming soon I know,
>   Coming back to this earth to reign;
> And His weary pilgrims will to glory go,
>   When the Saviour comes again.

May our hearts indeed respond, "Even so, come, Lord Jesus."

Author Biography

HENRY ALLAN IRONSIDE, one of the twentieth century's greatest preachers, was born in Toronto, Canada, on October 14, 1876. He lived his life by faith; his needs at crucial moments were met in the most remarkable ways.

Though his classes stopped with grammar school, his fondness for reading and an incredibly retentive memory put learning to use. His scholarship was well recognized in academic circles with Wheaton College awarding an honorary Litt.D. in 1930 and Bob Jones University an honorary D.D. in 1942. Dr. Ironside was also appointed to the boards of numerous Bible institutes, seminaries, and Christian organizations.

"HAI" lived to preach and he did so widely throughout the United States and abroad. E. Schuyler English, in his biography of Ironside, revealed that during 1948, the year HAI was 72, and in spite of failing eyesight, he "gave 569 addresses, besides participating in many other ways." In his eighteen years at Chicago's Moody Memorial Church, his only pastorate, every Sunday but two had at least one profession of faith in Christ.

H. A. Ironside went to be with the Lord on January 15, 1951. Throughout his ministry, he authored expositions on 51 books of the Bible and through the great clarity of his messages led hundreds of thousands, worldwide, to a knowledge of God's Word. His words are as fresh and meaningful today as when first preached.

The official biography of Dr. Ironside, *H. A. Ironside: Ordained of the Lord*, is available from the publisher.

The Written Ministry of H.A. Ironside

EXPOSITIONS

Joshua
Ezra
Nehemiah
Esther
Psalms (1-41 only)
Proverbs
Song of Solomon
Isaiah
Jeremiah
Lamentations
Ezekiel
Daniel
The Minor Prophets
Matthew
Mark
Luke
John
Acts
Romans
1 & 2 Corinthians
Galatians
Ephesians
Philippians
Colossians
1 & 2 Thessalonians
1 & 2 Timothy
Titus
Philemon
Hebrews
James
1 & 2 Peter
1, 2, & 3 John, Jude
Revelation

DOCTRINAL WORKS

Baptism
Eternal Security of the Believer
Letters to a Roman Catholic Priest
The Holy Trinity
Wrongly Dividing the Word of Truth
Death and Afterward
Holiness
The Levitical Offerings
Not Wrath But Rapture
The Unchanging Christ

HISTORICAL WORKS

The Four Hundred Silent Years
A Historical Sketch of the Brethren Movement

Other works by the author are brought back into print from time to time. All of this material is available from your local Christian bookstore or from the publisher.

LOIZEAUX

A Heritage of Ministry . . .

Paul and Timothy Loizeaux began their printing and publishing activities in the farming community of Vinton, Iowa, in 1876. Their tools were rudimentary: a hand press, several fonts of loose type, ink, and a small supply of paper. There was certainly no dream of a thriving commercial enterprise. It was merely the means of supplying the literature needs for their own ministries, with the hope that the Lord would grant a wider circulation. It wasn't a business; it was a ministry.

Much has changed in the years since then. Manuscripts are prepared on sophisticated computers, books are printed on high-speed web presses or published as electronic databases, and orders are phoned in toll-free or transmitted to us online. *But the essence of our work has not changed.*

Our Foundation Is the Word of God

We stand without embarrassment on the great fundamentals of the faith: the inspiration and authority of Scripture, the deity and spotless humanity of our Lord Jesus Christ, His atoning sacrifice and resurrection, the indwelling of the Holy Spirit, the unity of the church, the second coming of the Lord, and the eternal destinies of the saved and lost.

Our Mission Is to Help People Understand God's Word

We are not in the entertainment business. We only publish books we believe will be of genuine help to God's people, both through the faithful exposition of Scripture and practical application of its principles to contemporary need.

Faithfulness to the Word and consistency in what we publish have been hallmarks of Loizeaux for generations. And that means when you see the name Loizeaux on the outside, you can trust what is on the inside. That is our promise to the Lord...and to you.

If Paul and Timothy were to visit us today they would still recognize the work they began in 1876. Because some very important things haven't changed at all...this is still a ministry.